The story of
DODGER'S
of Norwich

Ronnie Green
and Dawn Castle-Green

Edited by Matthew Williams

First published 2018
by Curran Publishing
on behalf of SCT Books
75 Christchurch Road, Norwich NR2 3NG
info@smartcycletraining.co.uk

ISBN 978-0-9931603-2-5

Typeset in Sabon and Avenir by
Curran Publishing Services Ltd, Norwich, UK

Manufactured in the UK by Imprint Digital, Exeter

Main cover illustrations front & rear: stills taken from 1952 British Pathé's *The
Norwich Dodgers Penny Farthing Club* filmed at Newmarket Road. Colour has
been added to the original black & white images.

Contents

Figure 1 Eastward view down Chapel Street through a wheel, early 1950s

Foreword

There is a name over a corner property in 21st-century Norwich which refers to a dynasty once famous across the world. Sitting on Cambridge Street near the old hospital, it simply says DODGER'S.

For those of us who live in or around the city the chances are you will know where it is and who I am writing about. And so do those from farther afield. 'Where do you come from?' people would ask in far-flung corners of the globe. If the reply was Norwich then the follow-up question could well have been, 'Do you know Dodger?'

We are talking Dodger – the bike boy. Once met, never forgotten. Everybody seemed to know the dear old Dodger, and even if you had never actually met him you will probably have heard of him.

The Dodgers – there was more than one – were among the greatest characters the Fine City has ever produced. Stories about the extraordinary Kerrison clan who were a feature of city life for decades are legendary. 'Did you hear about the time Dodger did ...?' Or, 'What about when he told that chap from the council to ...?' Wonderful.

Now, at last, something has happened which I doubted I would ever see. It is a book dedicated to our Dodger's and detailing the impact the family had on life in the city and across the county for so many years. Family members Ronnie Green and Dawn Castle-Green have got together with the writing cyclist Matthew Williams to come up with a book to cherish. A galaxy of great memories, stories and rare photographs.

What a task! What a tribute! A truly marvellous read and a must for anyone interested in Norwich folk, who possess a sense of humour like no other. And who know how to make a bob or two.

As the original Dodger, George Henry Kerrison, announced many years back: A NORWICH CELEBRITY. WHY AM I KNOWN? BECAUSE I AM AN INTERESTING PERSON, ONCE SEEN & HEARD, I'M NEVER FORGOTTEN.

How true. They don't make 'em like Dodger any more ...
Enjoy the book.

Derek James

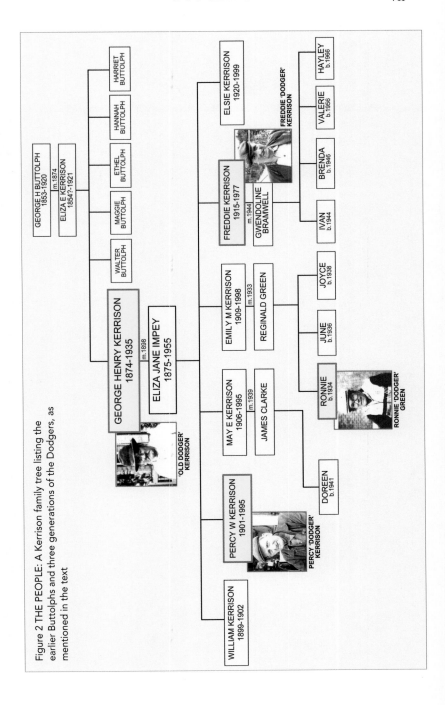

Figure 2 THE PEOPLE: A Kerrison family tree listing the earlier Buttolphs and three generations of the Dodgers, as mentioned in the text

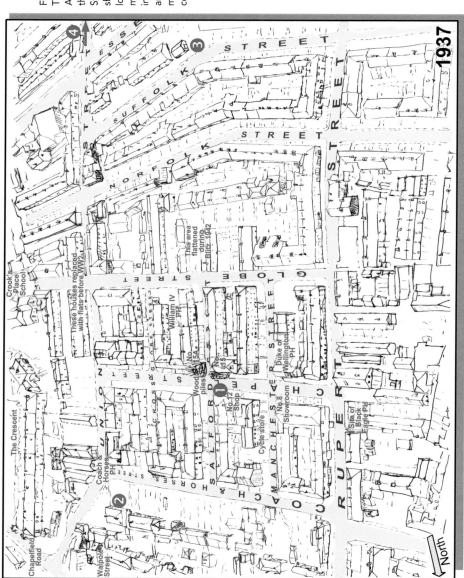

Figure 3
THE PLACES:
Aerial view of
the Chapel
Street area
showing key
locations
mentioned
in the text,
and a modern
map for
comparison

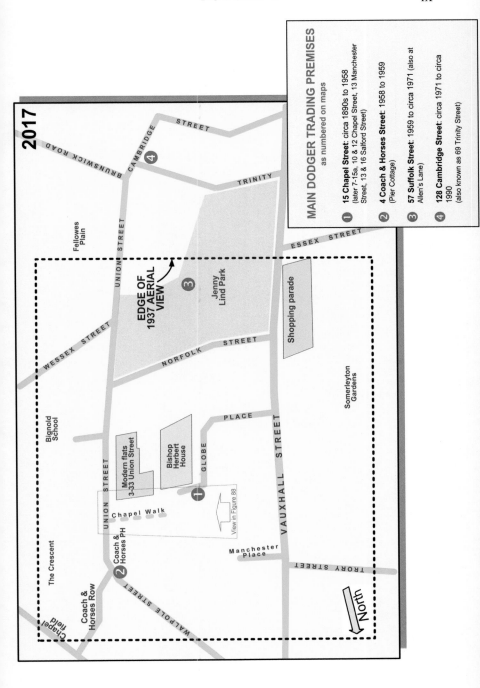

2017

MAIN DODGER TRADING PREMISES
as numbered on maps

1 **15 Chapel Street**: circa 1890s to 1958 (later 7-15a, 10 & 12 Chapel Street, 13 Manchester Street, 13 & 16 Salford Street)

2 **4 Coach & Horses Street**: 1958 to 1959 (Pier Cottage)

3 **57 Suffolk Street**: 1959 to circa 1971 (also at Allen's Lane)

4 **128 Cambridge Street**: circa 1971 to circa 1990 (also known as 69 Trinity Street)

BRUNSWICK ROAD

CAMBRIDGE STREET

TRINITY

Fellowes Plain

ESSEX STREET

EDGE OF 1937 AERIAL VIEW

Jenny Lind Park

UNION STREET

WESSEX STREET

NORFOLK STREET

Shopping parade

Somerleyton Gardens

Bignold School

PLACE

Modern flats 3-33 Union Street

Bishop Herbert House

GLOBE

VAUXHALL STREET

The Crescent

UNION STREET

Chapel Walk

View in Figure 88

Coach & Horses PH

Manchester Place

Coach & Horses Row

WALPOLE STREET

TROWY STREET

Chapel field

North

Figure 4 Dawn Castle-Green and Ronnie
Green during an epic series of rides they
made in 1996 to visit all the churches in
Norfolk

Introduction

This is a story about a hardworking Norwich family who in their way were working-class heroes, but who, after many years of graft, became a wealthy and rather secretive landowning dynasty.

The authors are both part of the story, Dawn unknowingly entering as the wife of arguably the last holder of the title 'Dodger',[1] Ronald Frederick Green – he became her second husband in 1993. It was only during the 1990s that she started becoming aware of the remarkable background to this family and the part it played in the history of Norwich.

The essence of the story is this. Ronnie's grandfather George Henry Kerrison lived in a poor Norwich suburb and set himself up as a dealer in the 1890s. Through hard work he succeeded in building a business largely based on selling coal to the neighbourhood and bicycles to the people of the city, to whom he was known as Dodger. He began to acquire local houses, and by the time of his death in 1935 owned a large property portfolio which was further expanded by his sons during and after the Second World War. They rebranded the cycle business as Dodger's and achieved national fame through a film made in the 1950s featuring their collection of antique bicycles. Later that decade and after a hard fight with the city council, the firm's longstanding base was compulsorily purchased as part of a redevelopment project. The business continued trading from a sequence of other shop locations, but eventually closed in the early 1990s with the retirement of Percy Dodger Kerrison in his nineties.

Why is it important to tell this story?

It is interesting at a number of levels, not least as a piece of social history: if not quite a rags-to-riches story, there was wealth and a successful business handed on to the next generation, followed later by a slow decline eventually leading to closure. Along the way there is a prolonged battle of wills between a 'man of the people' and a strongly socialist local authority.

From a transportation viewpoint, the tale takes us from the end of the cycle craze in the nineteenth century right through the period of mass cycling and beyond into the present era. The Dodger collection of vintage bikes was second to none. And for

---

1   *at least in some angling circles.*

those who enjoy local history, Dodger's domain was originally one of the earliest areas of residential expansion outside the city walls and was recorded in detail in his photographs. This area was severely damaged by enemy action in the 1940s, then around 1960 it was entirely erased and replanned, raising questions about modern architecture, and about civic methods and motives.

The above strands have occasionally been featured in local newspaper articles, and even in a regional TV programme, but have not previously been considered together, or in any depth.

Of course, we also have a particular family's history through three or more generations, which is itself a fascinating account of personalities and personal circumstances. These help us to understand decisions that were made and the way that things turned out.

From time to time certain members of the family started to record their recollections, and these notes have been invaluable. However, it was not really possible to address the full story until the last child of George Henry Kerrison had died in 1999 and a considerable quantity of archive material then became available. It was Ronnie who persuaded Dawn to take on the job of writing the history of this characterful family – which she willingly agreed to do. It quickly became clear what a daunting task it was.

We have tried to describe in words the stages in the journey through over a hundred years of history. Ronnie has plenty of stories to tell. For Dawn, it is the photographs that tell even more than the words can say, which is why we have included plenty of illustrations. Most of them are in black and white, which may give a stark impression but one which may help reflect the 'no-nonsense' approach of the past. In our present more nuanced, multicoloured digital age, they remind us of a monochrome era that is now gone.

For Dawn, the juxtaposition of image and word is a lifetime obsession, and in finding the Dodger's archive while undertaking a cultural studies course, she discovered a priceless resource. The work soon became absorbing, and the interest never-ending. This is certainly enhanced by Ronnie adding a selection of his vividly told stories.

It has been a great challenge for us all to bring the various threads together to form a coherent tapestry but one which keeps its rich texture. The hope is it fairly conveys not only the story of a previously well-known Norwich family, but also a social history deeply rooted in the places we think we know.

Ronnie Green, Dawn Castle-Green
and Matthew Williams
January 2018

Acknowledgements

The authors and editor would like to express thanks to all those who have contributed to this account of the Dodgers, whether by anecdote or documentary information.

The starting point was written material originally left by Elsie and Percy Kerrison. This was supplemented by further research made by third-generation family members including Joyce, June, Ronnie and Doreen, some of which were earlier attempts at compiling a Dodgers history. The editor is grateful for being given access to these notes and for the kindness and cooperation of other family members including Ivan Kerrison, Hayley Kerrison-Wright and Joyce's husband Michael Henry.

Generous assistance in assimilating the history of Norwich cycle shops was given by Richard Freeman. The help of staff of Norfolk Heritage Centre is acknowledged in locating material used in Chapters 9 and 10.

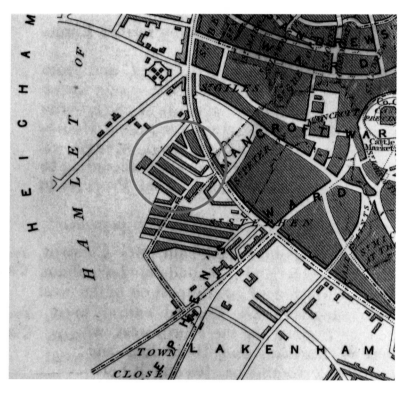

Figure 5 Extract from 1837 map showing contemporary extent of development outside Norwich city wall, with Union Place highlighted in red

1

A Crook's Place lad

The Dodgers story is one that straddles most of the twentieth century, but has its roots firmly in the nineteenth century. We could begin with the birth in 1874 of the individual who started it all – George Henry Kerrison.

He was born on 5 March in North Elmham, near Dereham. The first thing we notice from the register of births is that it was his *mother's* surname that is Kerrison. This is because he was a child born out of wedlock, which was not particularly unusual then but would nevertheless have been associated with a certain stigma in late Victorian times. In fact, George's mother Eliza Elizabeth did go on to marry his father George Henry Buttolph, who was from Wymondham, a few months later in 1874, but George's surname remained Kerrison.[2]

Were it not for this unplanned turn of events, the Dodgers would have been largely Buttolphs rather than Kerrisons. A family tree is given in Figure 2 at the front of this book.

Notwithstanding his illegitimacy, George was given fore-names identical to his father's to go in front of his mother's surname. Confusingly, his name was actually recorded as George Henry Buttolph by the enumerators on the 1881 and 1891 census records while he was still growing up as part of his father's household (by then residing in Norwich), probably to avoid the trouble of explaining why the eldest child bore a different surname from his siblings. By the time of the 1901 census, he had reached adulthood with his own household and had reverted to his proper name George Henry Kerrison, as recorded on his birth record.

On the face of it, the child George Henry Kerrison was an

---

2 A number of receipts found among the family papers dating up to the late 1920s relating to bought items are mysteriously made out to George Henry Buttolph. It is possible this was Dodger Kerrison passing himself off as a Mr Buttolph for some reason, using his 'alternative' surname. Another explanation is that purchases were indeed made by his father, who was probably helping out with his son's business until his death in 1920, but that does not adequately explain later receipts bearing that name. We do know that one of Dodger's siblings Walter Buttolph ran an ice cream business nearby and helped George out from time to time.

ordinary boy in Norwich who went to his local school, Crook's Place School. No, this was not a school for educating criminals as some might mischievously suggest, but an educational institution that bore the name of an early nineteenth-century gentleman from Manchester, John Crook.

It was John Crook who with others had been responsible for the development (as early as the 1820s) of that part of Norwich lying directly outside the city wall in the area of Chapelfield, on the south-west side of the city (see Figure 5). This area had previously been used for the extraction of a thin layer of brick earth, leaving undulations and slopes where layers of sandy clay had been dug out. The land was subsequently laid out with neat rows of houses, and of necessity provided with a chapel and a school for the improvement of the poorer classes. The school has survived to this day as Bignold Primary School, but most of the original buildings occupying streets that abutted it to the south and west have long since disappeared following repeated phases of redevelopment. An aerial view showing the area is presented for reference near the front of this book (Figure 3).[3]

George Henry Kerrison was the eldest child, with a brother and three sisters (all Buttolphs of course), their father earning a living as a confectioner. They grew up living at 15 Chapel Street, part of an early to mid-nineteenth-century building of up to three storeys, where the top rooms (garrets) were originally intended for use for weaving or other home work requiring good daylight. The rest of the complex, known as Manchester Buildings, was built in the form of a square, and incorporated a limited number of latrines located in the centre at the back, for the amenity of the large number of residents. It stood in a densely inhabited block bounded by Union Street, Norfolk Street, Rupert Street (now Vauxhall Street) and Walpole Street, forming the central part of Union Place which was the next district north-westwards from Crook's Place.

'Dodger' was allegedly the nickname given to the boy by his mother, for it is said that when missing he would often be found in a neighbour's yard, and his mother would invariably say 'Come on you little Dodger.'[4]

---

3   Only vestiges of the original roads remain today as the area has since been subject to such comprehensive redevelopment, in some cases involving more than one phase of rebuilding.

4   The name stuck for the rest of his life: everyone locally knew Dodger (it is a most

Figure 6 George Kerrison and Eliza Impey on their wedding day, 3 October 1898

Figure 7 George and Eliza's wedding certificate

As a young boy George kept tame rats, with which he used to tease a pretty dark-haired school girl. The picture of George that emerges at this stage is of a cheeky and lively young lad with an innate ability to do his own thing, and also to win the attention of others. That girl later became his wife. Her name was Eliza Impey, and she was the daughter of a gardener originally from the Hethersett area. She was born in the same area that George grew up in (she was living at Cross Globe Street), and thus also went to the same school. You can see that for people such as these, life tended to be quite localised.

While George and Eliza were courting, he was working in the family business as a milk seller, and Eliza had entered domestic service at Tuckswood Farm House. The couple were married at St Stephen's Church in October 1898 (Figure 6), at which point the certificate records George's occupation as a mineral water maker. His father's name and occupation are noticeably left blank (Figure 7). Their address was shown as 72 King Street, Crook's Place (later known as Shadwell Street).

Before long a first child was on the way, and the 1901 census records they had set up home in 15 Chapel Street, apparently made possible by George's parents and siblings having moved along the road to 10 Manchester Street. The birth of their first child must have concentrated his mind on how the young couple and family were going to make ends meet.

suitable name for a general dealer), and the title was later passed on to his son – at which point George Henry then became Old Dodger.

2

The makings of a business

Hard times

To understand the Kerrisons' situation it is necessary to bear in mind the general economic condition of the city of Norwich towards the end of the nineteenth century and at the beginning of the twentieth.

By the time we get to the period after the industrial revolution, Norwich was according to Pevsner the most poverty-stricken city in England. Many people had moved from rural areas into the city. There were hundreds of densely populated yards throughout the city where people lived with what came to be recognised as completely inadequate water supply or sewerage arrangements. Not surprisingly there were several health epidemics including smallpox, typhoid and cholera. Although there was much concern and hand-wringing by government and local authority, large-scale attempts to remedy the situation had still not yet reached the poorest areas by the time the rebuilt Norfolk & Norwich Hospital opened in 1881.

By the end of the nineteenth century the previously vital weaving industry in Norwich had largely gone, and despite diversification into shoemaking and other labour-intensive industries, even those who could find work found it difficult to earn enough. The only legal way for a determined person to succeed was via hard graft, and in particular to provide a service which the people needed. For most, it was a matter of survival.

Living conditions in the early nineteenth-century tenements of Union Place were not ideal, but at least they were built on higher ground at the edge of the built-up area. Life in the back-to-back cottages of some of the damp lower-lying areas of the old city centre must have been more miserable, especially during the great floods of 1878 and 1912.

Dodgers' origins

George had a wife and family to support. He may have been small in stature, but he was big in personality and determination, and

Dodger made work happen. From mineral water maker he extended his talents, and is said also to have gone around cleaning silver cutlery and boots in the Newmarket and Unthank Road areas before setting himself up as a general dealer.

At some stage, he must have identified the business opportunity afforded by there being a coal yard 600 yards to the east in Queens Road (Figure 8).[5] He would source coal from there to re-sell alongside wood during the winter, and see what else he could do in the summer.

And so we again see George's strong entrepreneurial spirit coming to the fore, combining a capacity for sheer hard work with an eye for marketing.

Conjure up the image from the 1900s: Dodger with orange rope round his chest, a London barrow loaded with half a ton (10 cwt) of coal and with the aid of his son Percy (still just a lad), pulling the barrow down Queens Road, along Chapel Field Road, up Union Street, along Chapel Street, and home. What a man!

Later on George acquired a donkey (Figure 9), then eventually a pony, replaced in time by a mule[6] and again another pony, all to assist in moving the coal and other materials (Figure 10). He also acquired a number of flat-rail hand barrows for shifting smaller loads.

His practice was to weigh the coal on scales in his small front garden, filling square biscuit tins with one stone of coal, offered at 2d a time, later 3½d. In due course he enclosed his garden by building a shed round it so he could work 'in the dry'.

Along with coal for fires came a demand for wood as kindling to start them. George needed to find a source for wood that he could store, cut up and re-sell. We know he was working with others to clear fallen trees using traction engines (Figure 11), but this may not have provided the ideal material for kindling.

He therefore made his way to Caley's, the huge factory on the opposite side of Chapelfield Road, and did a deal to buy old mineral-water wood bases (Figure 12). These bases were strongly wired together and actually took considerable work to

---

5   These days this site is occupied by a supermarket, but it was previously rail sidings – where coal was tipped from trucks brought in along a short branch from the London line that ran along what is now Lakenham Way (this railway line ran to Victoria Station, opened in 1849).

6   The mule was called Lord Nelson, having only one eye. We have a receipt dated 1919 for the pony that replaced it – see Figure 10.

Figure 8 The coal yard at Queens Road, pictured in 1986 shortly before it closed

convert into large bundles of wood. A blackboard on the wall at Chapel Street had chalked on it 'Tell your mother we sell bundles of wood, two a penny', i.e. they sold for halfpenny a bundle.

George also went to the Maypole cake shop in St Stephens Street and bought their wooden boxes for conversion to firewood. There is a tale about Dodger which was re-told within the family. On one occasion with his young son Percy and a flat-rail barrow, he loaded a large number of these wooden boxes to

Figure 9 Old Dodger standing behind the donkey, pictured in front of the wood pile. On the left is his brother Walter Buttolph, holding a large cross-cut saw.

Figure 10 Receipt for a pony purchased in 1919

Figure 11 Photo dating from just before the First World War showing George Kerrison on the right, and young Percy at the controls of a traction engine

take back to Chapel Street. Boy Percy was getting bored waiting and hung on the back of the barrow but suddenly it tipped up, throwing the stack of boxes off, which immediately blocked the narrow street, causing an obstruction to the trams. In those days one tram went up St Stephens Street while one tram went down (Figure 13), and you can imagine the commotion. Percy was chased round the barrow by his father and

Figure 12 Receipt in the name of Mr Buttolph for the purchase in 1919 of what on an accompanying document are described as 'old wood blocks'

Figure 13
View down
St Stephen's
Street in the
1930s

given a backhander – for of course he was held to blame – while all the time the driver of the tram was furiously ringing his bell.[7]

It was hard work in the years before and after the First World War, but Dodger's business progressed. More and more old wood was collected, sometimes as long planks which were sawn into smaller pieces and stockpiled in an ever-increasing wood pile outside their home on the corner at No. 15 Chapel Street

---

7   At this time in the early twentieth century the street was only 17 feet wide and always crowded with people, barrows and horses, and a few cars of early design. There were also of course many cycles, but with tram lines in place, there could be difficulties: once a cycle wheel was in the tram lines there was no getting out of them except to fall off.

(Figure 14). In time, he must have made and saved enough money to start acquiring neighbouring houses, probably starting with what became known as No.15a on the opposite corner of Chapel Street across Salford Street, where another wood pile accumulated (Figure 15).

An established business

Dodger Kerrison had become increasingly well known across the city, and could be seen transporting all manner of items, in some cases deftly balanced on hand barrows or carts, as necessary to get the job done. He even used a sledge for deliveries in the snow.

In the early years he appeared quite smartly dressed in a bowler hat and waistcoat even when wearing a sack apron, but later he wore a light coat, an occasional soft hat and rather severe expression below his moustache.

While the evidence suggests Dodger built his business mainly around supplying coal, coke and kindling, he continued to be engaged in general dealing, and from an early stage this included an interest in bicycles. We know this because there are surviving receipts for numerous bicycle repairs for him by S. Andrews, Peoples' Cycle Depot, Chapelfield Road dated 1897.[8] Furthermore, his entry on the 1901 census records his profession as 'Bicycle Agent', although it seems unlikely that this was his main source of income at that stage.

Years later, the family related another incident that had taken place when George was alive. It happened on a Saturday in Queens Road near the top of St Stephens, when a traction engine towing a timber trailer loaded with tree trunks was going up Queens Road. All of a sudden the coupling pin came adrift, and the trailer started to move backwards. Dodger was passing by with a load of coal on his pony and cart, returning from the coal yard in Queens Road, and was leading his pony towards Chapelfield Road. He was witnessing the makings of a disaster, had the trailer run into Ashworth's cake shop, with all those prams outside and people inside. Instantly he left his pony and cart with young Percy, and he chased after the runaway

8   This is one of the receipts in the name of Mr G Buttolph. We also have a receipt for 'lining pair of wheels' dated 1894, but as this also mentions 'painting and lettering name boards' this is more likely to refer to the wheels of a cart than a bicycle.

Figure 14 Northward view along Salford Street around 1911 showing the wood pile, with bowler-hatted George Kerrison on top and blond lad Percy perched on the edge

Figure 15 A different view from the previous one, this is looking westward along Chapel Street in the early 1920s showing wood piles at Nos.15 and 15a, on each side of Salford Street

trailer which had begun to gather momentum. He caught up to it at St Stephen's and grabbed the bar of the trailer, succeeding in turning it into Bull Lane, where it eventually came to rest. Disaster was averted. Dodger must have been considered a hero by those who witnessed the event, but he never received any thanks and Percy later noted how his father had been told by the owners he had no right to get involved.

George's eye for publicity

Alongside an innate ability for hard work and 'making it happen', it seems that the Kerrison genetic make-up included a talent for publicity and marketing.

This outlook had once got George into a spot of bother, as was again witnessed by son Percy, who was about 11 (and who retold the story later). This took place in the run-up to the general election before the First World War. George had a pony and cart and used it to carry sign boards advertising his cycle trade as he went about the city. He also sometimes used a bass drum, and the Liberal candidate had enlisted his help to display posters on the cart at Hay Hill and bang the drum to draw a crowd. Unfortunately, some Labour roughnecks in the crowd became violent. After taking the pony out of the shafts they tipped the cart over, tore the posters off, took the drum from George and put their feet through it. Thankfully nobody was injured, but the candidate assured George that if he got in at the vote, he would pay for the damage done to the cart and the drum. As it turned out the candidate did get in, but he never paid for the damage. From that day, Dodger senior never bothered voting.

He did however continue to promote his business through self-publicity. One of the portable advertising signboards he used later on read 'A NORWICH CELEBRITY. WHY AM I KNOWN? BECAUSE I AM AN INTERESTING PERSON, ONCE SEEN & HEARD I'M NEVER FORGOTTEN' (Figure 16).

Into the interwar years

Another story illustrates how hard George worked. On an occasion at the end of the First World War, Dodger had been given the job of moving a man's belongings from Norwich to his new home in Lowestoft, and set off with his pony pulling a cart of possessions piled high, once more accompanied by

Figure 16 George Kerrison and young daughter Elsie outside the Royal Standard
Cycle Depot, 12 Chapel Street, around 1926. Dressed smartly on the right is young
Alfie Warminger.

Percy. Having got only as far as Queen's Road, the poor pony
was unable to pull the load any further up the hill, so George
had a problem. By the roadside there was a group of dealers,
who had in their possession a mule they had evidently acquired
from an army sale at the Cattle Market. They agreed to sell
Dodger the mule for 30/- plus Dodger's pony. It was hitched up
and eventually the little party made it exhausted to Lowestoft,
where they had to await the arrival of the owner the next day.
They unloaded the cart, found a wash house at the back, filled
the copper with hay for the mule, then shoved him inside and
managed to close the door. They retired into the house to sleep,
and the following morning the house owner arrived looking less
than pleased. Rushing out, they found the mule had been unable
to turn around to get at his supper and in frustration had kicked
out at the wash house wall, bringing the whole side crashing
down. Needless to say, that particular customer refused to pay
for the removal job, and the sorry little party had to make their
way home. They later found the mule had only one eye.

Work continued and the cycle business expanded in the years
following the First World War. Although there is no specific listing
of him as a cycle dealer in the 1914 *Jarrolds Directory* and his
1915 national registration card merely had him down as a 'coal
hawker', it is clear that George had a significant amount of bi-

cycle business by 1919, as we have a receipt bearing that date for a number of inner tubes from Dunlop Rubber Company. In the archive is also a memo dated 1921 from F C Lusher of 48–50 King Street who sold cycles and prams, and were evidently responding to an enquiry from George about doing cycle business with them.[9] The 1924 *Kelly's Directory* simply records 'George H. Kerrison' at no. 15 Chapel Street as a private address, but in the 1925 edition his business appears as GH & P Kerrison, cycle agents, incorporating the initial of Percy. It may be because of his preoccupation with bicycles at this time that he was paying a cartage contractor (Henry Fulcher of Orchard Street) to move numerous of loads of wood to Globe Street and deliver coal to other addresses.

In due course, as turnover continued to grow, there came to be two businesses in the name of G H & P Kerrison: cycles one side of the street centred around no. 12 Chapel Street (which was bought in 1926), and wood, coal, props, linen posts, pea-sticks (and the rest) on the other side centred around nos 15 & 15a Chapel Street.

Many a local child was able to earn money by chopping sticks for Dodger (Figure 17). One person later remembered being paid ½d a biscuit tin, but also Dodger habitually shaking the tin and saying, 'You can get a few more in here.'

Local youngsters would hire bikes for 1d an hour, but sometimes keep them for many hours before sending them flying down Chapel Street to come to rest at Dodger's, then run off. Worse, there were four or five local gangs of boys who tried to terrorise the neighbourhood and sometimes got hold of the bikes which didn't come back. From an early time it was Percy's job to search for the abandoned cycles in the surrounding area, often finding them in the river at Harford Bridge or even hanging from telegraph posts. By around 1930, the hire charge had risen to 2d an hour, as recalled 65 years later by a writer to the newspaper who regularly hired bikes at that time as a 10-year-old.

A story from then was related by former PC106 Arthur Edmunds of no. 5 Beat, who found a penny farthing bike abandoned in the city centre one night. He thought he would road-test it but only succeeded in crashing into the window of Mark Antonio's fish shop at the bottom of Goat Lane. He had to agree

9 Lusher's seems to have disappeared shortly afterwards.

Figure 17
George, Elsie
and young
helpers,
chopping wood
ouside the
shop, around
1926

to pay 9d for the repair of the window, at 1d a week. On taking the penny farthing back to Dodger's, PC Edmunds cautioned him for having a bike with defective brakes. He also recalled how the police used to deliver a list of stolen cycles to all dealers, and they of course always included Dodger's.

We have seen that one aspect of the business was hiring out the flat barrows which were useful for carrying furniture when local people were moving house (Figure 18). In the late 1920s the hire charge for borrowing a barrow was 4d an hour. The following recollection is from rather later, in 1935:

About to be married, I had collected a few odds and ends of furniture at my lodgings in Highland Avenue and had to have them taken to our newly acquired house in George Borrow Road. How was I to do it? My landlady's son had the answer. 'Get in touch with Dodger Kerrison.' I found him in a yard full of all sorts of bits of wood and spoke to an elderly man, who was seated on a box cutting up wood for kindling. A date was arranged for the transportation.

Figure 18 Flat
barrows
pictured
stored
outside 7
Chapel Street,
around 1950

Dodger turned up with a flat handcart and a throng of children. We loaded up, he got between the shafts and off we went up Highland Road. I was young and mildly embarrassed by the interest taken by bystanders in our progress. The embarrassment was to increase when we reached Colman Road and turned right down the slope. Dodger, who wore plimsolls as I recall, broke into a trot, as did his escort of boys. I, who was showing the way, had to run to keep up the pace. We turned left into George Borrow Road and all was well. I asked Dodger how much I owed him. 'Half a crown, Guv'nor.'

It is evident that from not long after the First World War the Kerrisons had begun systematically to invest in property, and over the years they acquired freeholds of a number of adjoining addresses in the vicinity and elsewhere. These were often bought at auction, such as one we know they attended at the Royal Hotel in July 1920 run by Hanbury Williams to sell freehold dwelling-houses in Salford Street and Chapel Street. There was also investment by the family in improvements to the buildings, using local builders such as G. W. Gooch of Kimberley Street, T. Gill of Trinity Street and Anderson's of Park Lane.

Around 1926, George Henry managed to acquire the redundant Royal Standard public house at No. 12 Chapel Street. This stood at the corner of Salford Street directly across Chapel Street from his home at No. 15, and for a time after closure it had been used as a dairy. This he turned into the Royal Standard Cycle Depot. In 1934, with his sons' close involvement, he completely rebuilt the property next door (No. 12) to create additional show-room space, later using the wall spaces for advertising (Figure 19).

In the mid-1920s he was one of the first people in Norwich to acquire a motor scooter, and this he fitted out with advertising boards (Figure 20).[10] The bicycle business was obviously succeeding, for example in 1930 he was selling bicycles to Norwich Electric Tramways Company.

George's son Percy was increasingly entrusted to look after the cycle trade while his father continued to oversee the business of wood, coal and other fuel. In due course he was joined by his brother Freddie, who was 15 years younger than him. In the end, Percy took complete charge of bicycles, and Freddie came to be the one who delivered the coal. Other kinds of fuel supplied by Dodger's included paraffin, and petrol for motorbikes at around 4d for half a gallon.

---

10 This was a rear-engined ABC 'Skootamota' machine , now in North Walsham Motorcycle Museum.

Figure 19 View of Royal Standard from across Chapel Street, with Kerrisons ouside, 1935

If you were attempting to pass along the street (where there was no footway), you would in all likelihood have encountered busy activity filling the road among the chickens, the dogs and children playing.[11] There would be the chopping of wood,

11 There is said to have been a one-legged duck that roamed the street and a bantam cockerel that chased people.

Figure 20 Old Dodger and his early motor scooter, with Elsie (right) and her friend Popsie, around 1926

testing of bicycles, loading or unloading of barrows, motorcycles or vehicles, as well as people in conversation or workmen
in the midst of repairs to buildings or fencing.

Dodger's untimely death

George Henry Kerrison, the original Dodger, died unexpect-
edly on 28 September in tragic circumstances, at the age of
just 61. His daughter Elsie Kerrison later recorded the precise
circumstances of her father's death in a letter drafted to the local
newspaper:

*My dad was killed by a sewer rat. The corporation men were doing the
sewer in Cross Globe Street, when a rat ran out and into a woman's
garden. Dad was well known for his willingness to help people and
when a neighbour screamed out to him, he went to her aid. The rat
ran past him and instinctively he put his foot out and stood on its tail.
It turned round on him and bit his leg before he killed it. He did go
to the hospital, but in time the poison worked into his system. There
was no penicillin at that time otherwise his life might have been saved.*

It is sadly ironic that the lad who once used to keep tame rats
ended up meeting a premature end following an encounter with
a rat of rather a different kind. The cause of death was officially
recorded as uraemia and nephritis (kidney failure), as a result
of Weil's disease (a bacterial infection). It must have been very
painful and unpleasant. It is not known how long he may have
waited before attending hospital, but it is said that both his sons
had been away in Wymondham that day bidding for a house
and there was therefore no one else to look after the business.

His daughter went on to note, '*He was not a Lord Mayor or
a civil dignitary, just a working man, yet such was his way of
life that there were close on 400 people at his graveside.*' These
people came to show respect for this hard-working hero whose
generosity had ended up costing him his life.

Another reason Old Dodger was so liked by the community
was that he had often allowed local people have paraffin and
coal in return for their pawn tickets. After his death a large
pot of these tickets were found which had evidently not been
redeemed, meaning he was never paid.

A collection was made in the days following his death from
Chapel Street neighbours (by a Mrs Rice and Mrs Duffy) for

a floral token. It raised £1 5s 3d. The undertakers were G. W. Gooch & Son of Kimberley Street, who charged £15 7s 6d including for a hearse and pair and five broughams. The headstone was supplied the following year by Arthur Potter of Rupert Street at a cost of £31 3s 6d (Figure 21).

Figure 21 The Kerrison family plot at Earlham Cemetery: George & Eliza's grave, pictured in 2017. Later graves behind are those of their children Percy, Emily, Elsie and Freddie.

3

Old Dodger and the Kerrison family

Over the 22 years that followed George Henry's marriage to Eliza back in 1898, they produced six children (the family tree is on Figure 2). The first one, a boy called William, died when he was only 3 years old. The second child was Percy.[12] They then had two girls, first May then Emily, and another boy Frederick (or Freddie). Their youngest child was a girl Elsie, who was in the course of time the person responsible for writing down some of the detail about the life of her father as related in the previous chapter.

From a detached twenty-first century viewpoint it is possible to look back at the dynamics of families like the Kerrisons who built businesses in the nineteenth and early twentieth centuries, and to recognise the significance of gender at the time. From the start everything must have revolved around George Henry as the male head of the household: he bore the responsibility and took all the important decisions. The family's economic survival depended on activity requiring much manual labour (not least the constant chopping of wood), and every blood member of the family, male or female, was expected to work hard for the good of the business. While everyone had their say, it is unlikely that anyone questioned what was by default the male right to decide who did what and when.

This is why, when it came to who would eventually follow George in the second stratum of the family, it was always going to be his elder surviving son, Percy. From an early age he was working alongside (but of course subordinate to) his father in most Kerrison activities, later being trusted with errands and other tasks. He went on to become the second Dodger, continuing the business for many years after Old Dodger had died. We will look at that progression in later chapters.

Needless to say Eliza Kerrison, George's wife, did play a vital role over three decades in supporting her husband and helping to bring up the family, after the early setback of losing their first child. After she was widowed, she continued to live in the

---

12 Percy was eventually to take over the name of Dodger from his father, who then became Old Dodger.

Figure 22 Eliza Kerrison, pictured in 1939

Chapel Street area and was herself supported in old age by her daughters (Figure 22). She is remembered as a kind and loving grandmother, but at the same time as one who had her own opinions and who continued to be a strong influence on her offspring and her grandchildren.

We will now mention in turn the various members of the Kerrison family (George and Eliza's five surviving children) and their role within the story.

Percy

Percy was the eldest surviving son in the second generation. He was also known within the family as 'Passy'. Having worked alongside his father in the firm from an early age, he was given responsibility for the bicycles side of the business while George was still alive. As discussed above, he was the obvious person to take over from his father when the time came.

In contrast to his later demeanour, Percy was known as a young man as 'a gay young thing' (Figure 23), prone to getting into scrapes. In 1924 he was asked for compensation from a Wymondham butcher after running down a sheep (Figure 24), and the same year he was summonsed for riding his motorbike in St Benedict's Street without a silencer. There are tales of summer evening trips on his Triumph motorbike to Dunston Common with young ladies on the pillion.[13]

Everybody expected him to marry his serious girlfriend, but this never happened. In the mid-1930s when his father died, things quickly took a more serious turn and he found himself

---

13 One unlikely tale he use to retell later was about having been marooned late at night at Dunston (with his young lady) after a flat tyre, allegedly caused by discarded gramophone needles discarded by picnickers. The girl's irate father apparently had to be shown the needles recovered from the tyre.

Figure 23 Percy, a studio portrait photo taken in the early 1920s

heading the family business. He ended up living the rest of his
life as a bachelor.

While Percy eventually emerged from the shadow of his well-
known and respected father Old Dodger, he probably never fully
got over the suddenness with which he had to take his mantle.

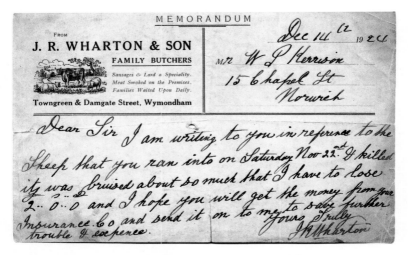

Figure 24 A note to Percy in 1924 demanding compensation following an incident in Wymondham

He retained a terror of rats as the direct result of the way in which his father had met his end. It was therefore not so much of a mantle he wore, as permanent leg protection.

Ronnie recalls an aspect of his uncle's personality:

When I first knew him, people already had given Percy a certain rude label, meaning he was a bit tight-fisted. For example, he once charged 1d for pumping someone's bike tyres up, and when this was questioned, he said he didn't charge for the pumping – but for the air that he could have breathed in.

Percy Kerrison came to epitomise the Dodgers in his outlook and attitudes. The name of the firm was an appropriate description for the ways in which much of the business was done. Penny-pincher or not, he undoubtedly went on to become one of the great Norwich characters. His role in the Dodgers story was a substantial one played out over nearly sixty years, and he continued to run the business right through to his early 90s. We will describe that in more detail in the chapters that follow.

May

The eldest daughter was christened Eliza, but she was called May to avoid confusion with her mother Eliza. She grew up in the bosom of the family and must have been closely involved in the

Figure 25 May Kerrison, with her younger sister Elsie and kitten, photographed in front of the shop around 1926

business in her early years (Figure 25). However, in due course she gained outside employment at Bally & Holdenstein's shoe factory in Princes Street. At the start of the Second World War she married James H. Clarke, who was a few years younger than her. While at Chapel Street she used to sell fruit that had been picked in the orchard behind the Wymondham house. They moved from Chapel Street to Bolingbroke Road in the late 1950s.

Emily

Emily was Old Dodger's second daughter, and grew up into a strong-willed young lady with fixed opinions. She remained a chip off the old block, no fool, and a hard worker – as had always been the Kerrison tradition – contributing to the family's income. Having grown up surrounded by wood she loved chopping sticks, and years later never passed a piece of wood in the street without taking it home.

Thanks to her sister May, she too found employment at Holdenstein's shoe factory in the late 1920s as a 'runner' keeping the machinists supplied with needles and cotton. She was given the nickname 'Felix' (after the cartoon cat) because of her athleticism up and down the stairs to the clickers' floor, and her ability to despatch the mice sometimes spotted in the factory.

In 1933 Emily married Reginald Green, a fish fryer at Mitchell's at the top of Grapes Hill. They lived at Willow Lane then at Salford Street, and three children followed before the onset of the Second World War. Life in Union Place changed abruptly after bombing in April 1942 – in fact they were lucky not to lose their lives as many did during the Blitz. The day after the biggest raid, Emily and her family were evacuated to Wymondham, first to Norwich Road then to Tuttles Lane. She later found a bungalow in Chapel Lane opposite the Chapel Bell public house, remaining there until 1947. She took her three young children daily to school at Browick Road, using a trailer towed behind her bicycle (Figure 26). She always said these were the happiest days of her life.

Emily taught herself to play the piano by ear, and was given a canteen piano by American servicemen when they left Deopham Green Airfield in 1945. Her ability to pick out a tune helped her earn extra cash over most of her lifetime. She was clever

Figure 26 Emily Green in 1943 at Chapel Bridge in Wymondham, with the three children in a trailer made by Percy, and Flossie the dog

with her hands, making money in her spare time by creating floral brooches, and husband Reggie also made woven placemats while he was serving in Gibraltar.

After the war, the family were re-housed back to Norwich at Beecheno Road, several miles from her old home. Looking after three children and working full-time at Bally's shoe factory, she wasn't able to see her Dodger family as much as she might have liked. However, by now she had been doing her 'own thing' for a number of years, and it is inevitable that the sense of Kerrison family solidarity that had ruled in the past was becoming undermined.

In Emily's branch we can see the effect of changing attitudes to 'family' in the mid twentieth century, exacerbated by the effects of war and displacement. A certain distance opened up from the 'core' members Elsie and Percy, who perhaps understandably became a little more secretive. Although Emily's daughter June later took on secretarial work for the business, she didn't have full access to names and addresses of Percy and Elsie's contacts. After Percy's death, Elsie would still not allow Ronnie and his wife Dawn to go upstairs or into her cellar where documents were stored.

Emily lived until the age of 89, passing away in 1998, a year before her younger sister Elsie.

Freddie

Frederick Kerrison had been born during the First World War, by which time his elder brother Percy was already playing his part in the family business. It seems inevitable that he grew up in the shadow not just of his father, but also of his brother, who was 15 years older than him. When George Henry died in 1935, Freddie was suddenly in at the deep end in regard to the solid fuel side of the business, which had by then had become quite busy and profitable. He was going to struggle to manage that on his own.

Elsie recalled that she was working in Brenner's Bazaar in St Stephen's Street, earning 12 shillings a week working long hours. Freddie asked her to help him in his side of the business, and she left the shop in order to work with her brother. Elsie already knew how to chop wood, make bundles of wood, weigh out stones of coal and fill pails with coke. She also took the orders for coal, with Freddie making the deliveries. The working hours were probably as least as long as they had been at Brenner's, probably less regular, and whether she still received hard cash in her pocket at the end of the week remains unknown.

The two brothers remained close (Figure 27), at least in terms of the management of their late father's businesses, which they had little choice but to inherit and continue trading. We have already seen how the activities were already essentially divided into two. While Percy continued to look after the cycles, Freddie dealt with the fuels side, which he ran with help from Elsie and others. However, once the Second World War arrived, Freddie signed up for service in the RAF, and was not around from late 1940, so it was left to Percy (who himself had joined the Home Guard and was an Air Raid Patrol warden) and to remaining family members to keep the fuels side of the business going.

Freddie married Gwendoline (known as Gwennie) in 1941, having met her in the NAAFI canteen, and they subsequently had a son. She remained in Norwich and is remembered selling toffee apples from their home at Manchester Street. In line with the family tradition, their son Ivan did subsequently start working in the business in the mid-1950s, but he left after a time. Being expected to go to work in that way was perhaps the norm for a

Figure 27 Percy and Freddie, outside the Royal Standard in the late 1930s. See also Figure 79.

family concern in former decades, but as a young man growing up in the middle of the twentieth century, Ivan was beginning to expect financial independence, and to find his own way. Freddie's RAF service in Yorkshire was spent in ground crew including loading bombs. Despite the supporting camaraderie of life on base, it seems he did not greatly enjoy the experience. He was discharged for health reasons in 1943 and returned to the family business. He was referred to as Fred 'Dodger' Kerrison, to avoid confusion with his brother. Once back, he became rather disillusioned with the state of the post-war city and by the moves towards compulsory purchase and relocation. He worked long days keeping the solid fuel business going and assisting Percy. Freddie died at the relatively early age of 61, the cause recorded as stroke and brochopneumonia.

After Freddie's death in 1977, Ivan and his mother Gwennie's direct involvement with the family business more or less ceased. They were regarded by Percy and Elsie as inheritors on the sidelines more than close family – Elsie had never really seen eye-to-eye with her sister-in-law even while her brother was alive. Living as near neighbours at Adelaide Street (Elsie at no.100, Gwennie at 104) became increasingly difficult, and it is not surprising that Gwennie sold her house two years later and moved away to Bowthorpe.[14]

In hindsight it can be said that Freddie's passing was a significant loss to the business in operational terms. While at the time it may have seemed everything was in his elder brother's capable hands, Percy of course had no child to bring into the firm in the same way that he had been brought in. The natural heir might perhaps have been Ronnie, Emily's son, but that was not to be as her branch had sided with Gwennie, and consequently Ronnie was never asked to work in the business. With no succession or youthful energy in line, Freddie's death was in a sense the beginning of the end of the business, although thanks to Percy's longevity it was to be many years before the Dodger's brand was gone for ever.

Ronnie does however have fond memories of his Uncle Freddie, who was to some extent a surrogate father while his own dad Reggie was away in the forces:

One time in the early 1940s I remember I was unwrapping a new bike

14 There was an unfortunate dispute later over the ownership of an antique car that had been in store since the 1950s. This was a chauffeur-driven Triumph Dolomite acquired from a lady in The Crescent, at a time when Freddie was teaching Percy to drive.

for my uncle, and in those days a crepe-like paper was all round the frame and the forks. The cycle was a child's three-wheeler tandem, colour pale blue. [I've never seen one like it before or since, and that child's tandem was either stolen or stored away in the late 1950s along with other cycles of Dodger's.] My Uncle Freddie told me to gather up all the paper from it and any old cardboard from empty boxes laying around. He said to put it all on a flat rail barrow and take it to Alfie Warminger's in Globe Street.[15] It was a bit of a push up Salford Street, and I couldn't see over the top of the barrow, me being only about 6 years old. The man there gave me sixpence (6d) for the paper and card. I was so pleased, as I'd never had 6d before. On getting back to Dodger's in Chapel Street, Freddie asked 'How much did you get?' and I proudly opened my palm. 'Sixpence,' I said. 'Good,' said Freddie, taking it out of my hand. 'Just enough for the hire of the barrow,' he said.

I never piped my eye when my parents or other relations died, except for my Uncle Freddie. Often he'd take me on his coal round in his Morris Eight. We'd go along Chapelfield Road stopping at the coffee stall on the left almost opposite the Champion Public House. He'd buy me a cake. We'd get the coal up at the Queens Road depot where Sainsbury's now is. We had a trailer on the back, and before that a motorbike and sidecar. Freddie also gave me my first fishing rod – and years later I went on to become Norwich & District angling champion.

I also remember Uncle Freddie once taking me to the Corn Hall in Exchange Street. They held boxing matches there as well as auctions. The roof was all glass held up with girders, and an auction was being held. I saw a pigeon on the girders, and said 'Freddie', pointing up to the pigeon 'Blimey,' said Freddie, 'You've just bid for a suite of furniture.' It was fortunate someone else put in another bid before the hammer fell!

Elsie

Elsie was the youngest of George Henry's children, arriving in 1920, and remained unmarried throughout her life (Figure 28). She did have her admirers, and it was said that at one stage Alfie Warminger was sweet on Elsie. However, in the event she spent all her life with the family, first with her parents, then with her mother Eliza, and then with her brother Percy right through until he moved into a nursing home.

Elsie grew up doing odd tasks for the family business as had her siblings, but like May she managed to get a job elsewhere at an early stage to bring in some cash. In a note written before her death, Elsie recalled how in 1935 she had been working in

---

15 Mr Warminger was a well-known Norwich coal merchant and entrepreneur.

Figure 28 Elsie Kerrison, a studio
portrait taken in the early 1930s

Brenner's Bazaar in St Stephen's, where she was a shop assistant.[16]

Elsie started work there in 1934 after she left school at 14 years of age. Her wage was 9/- a week (the older women received more, the top wage was 25/-) and the hours were 9am till 6.30pm. On Fridays it was 9am to 8pm, and on Saturdays it was 9am until 9pm. On Fridays and Saturdays she had to go to Deacon's fish shop (on the corner of Westlegate and Red Lion Street) to get chips for some of the assistants. There was also an exciting incident when a bullock appeared in the shop.[17]

At Christmastime she received 1/-, otherwise known as her box. She remembered one Christmas coming along the back of Coburg Street pleased with 10/- in her pocket, her week's wages after a very busy week.

Sometimes Mr Brenner himself would come into the shop to wander around and speak to the assistants, and Elsie liked him. In February 1936, all the staff were in shock when told of his death in a car accident. She and several other Norwich shop staff attended the funeral service in the Jewish synagogue.

She left Brenner's to assist her brother Freddie around the time their father died, and from then on maintained a continuous involvement in the business. During the Second World War, Elsie was exempted from service because she was looking after her aged mother, but she also helped to keep Freddie's side of the firm going when he was away in the RAF. After the war she lived with Percy at No. 100 Adelaide Street (Figure 29), and she dealt with much of the administrative work that must have been necessary to

---

16 She worked at the Brenner's Sixpenny Bazaar, rather than the Penny Bazaar which was farther down the street. This shop chain was quite well known as a producer of local postcards, and sold a range of other goods. It had been started by a Romanian entrepreneur called Max Brenner, who lived in the city and who had opened branches elsewhere in East Anglia.

17 The animal had escaped from one of the several slaughterhouses that were located in yards off St Stephen's; she wrote a letter to the Evening News in 1996 about this incident.

manage the collection of properties he had inherited or later acquired.[18]

Dawn comments:

Elsie's lifetime of involvement with the family business must have been a cross to bear at times, but also her pride and joy. How proud she must have been taking part in cycle cavalcades in the 1950s (see Chapter 6) – you can see that in some of the photographs. Being at the heart of the family helped protect her from the harsh winds of life, but it was not all sunshine later on when it came to all the trouble surrounding the compulsory purchases (see Chapter 7).

Figure 29 Elsie and elder brother Percy pictured at their temporary home, 18 Coach & Horses Street, late 1950s

Dawn believes the long and ultimately unsuccessful fight with the council during the 1950s (described in Chapter 7) had a damaging effect on Elsie, who probably never fully recovered from the effects of stress. She was subsequently sent away to have a break in the country. Later, after having moved to 98 Trinity Street, she kept folders of old photographs and took these with her on occasional stays in hospital to show fellow patients, as tangible reminders of all that her family had meant to her.

Elsie outlived all of her siblings and died in May 1999, this date being in effect the final end of the Kerrison business era. It triggered the division of the remaining family assets into several parcels under the terms of her will, but only after a considerable number of generous bequests had been made to various charities.

---

18 After Percy had retired in 1995, Elsie moved into one of those properties, a double-fronted end terrace house at no. 98 Trinity Street, which had originally been bought for letting in 1980.

4

Percy takes the mantle

The business must continue

Let us return to the year 1935. George's eldest son Percy must have been affected deeply by the unexpected and tragic loss of his father, but the business momentum continued because he was already a prime mover in expansion plans of the early 1930s.

He now had a widowed mother to look after, notwithstanding her reputation as ruling the roost, and suddenly life became more serious. And from then on, it is said he always made sure that his legs were protected by wearing cycle clips or tucking his trousers into his socks.[19]

Soon after their father's death, Percy and Freddie made a clearer division of the retail business into two parts, reflecting an informal separation that had developed while their father was alive. Percy was the one who received his father's mantle and eventually became fully Dodger in his own right. It was he who took care of the selling, repairing and hiring out of bicycles plus the related sales of parts and accessories. Freddie oversaw the storage, selling and distribution of coal, coke and wood.

These two sides of the business were never entirely separate, and the two brothers evidently provided support to each other as necessary. For example, a few years previously, Percy had acquired a powerful motorbike and sidecar, and this was used to move large loads of coal (Figure 30).[20] Conversely, Freddie remained the firm's expert on adjusting bicycle derailleur gears (as opposed to hub gears) and was often called on by Percy. Elsie was later at pains to say how she performed a unifying role in the years after their father's death, helping them both in their activities.

Percy was already used to negotiating property purchases long before his father died, and this continued apace. In 1936 Percy was evidently trying to buy the freeholds of 12, 14 and

---

19 This explanation for his customary leg attire for the remainder of the working life was divulged later in one of the Dick Joice *Bygones* film profiles on Percy.

20 These were often stacked on the sidecar and in a trailer. He once moved 10 cwt of coal balanced on a ladder lashed to the sidecar, and a picture of this feat found its way into the *Daily Mirror*. Sometimes rope was tied around the motorbike's rear wheel to get it to grip. Freddie later purchased a lorry for moving bags of coal, each of which weighed a hundredweight (1 cwt = 51kg).

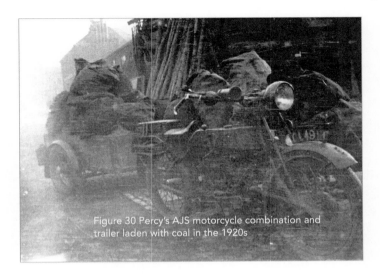

Figure 30 Percy's AJS motorcycle combination and trailer laden with coal in the 1920s

16 Manchester Street, but the owner was reluctant to sell (Percy finally succeeded in 1948). He already owned the first of a number of houses further along Chapel Street (Figure 31). In 1937 he bought several houses at Adelaide Street (this was twelve years before he acquired the house there to which he and Elsie eventually moved).

The selling and hiring of cycles also continued as before, and so did occasional attempts by unscrupulous customers to trick the Kerrisons. One correspondent with the newspaper admitted years later having hired a bike from Dodger's for 4d an hour, then keeping the hired bike and returning their old one instead, hoping this would not be noticed!

Figure 31 Houses at 16–24 Chapel Street and 18 Cross Globe Street, pictured in the 1930s

Chapel Street

The fact that Dodger lived on site in relation to his business meant he could offer the ultimate level of service to his customers – day and night, as well as being open on Sundays.

The geographical heart of the Dodgers' domain had for many years been at Chapel Street, but over time their sphere of control spread into adjacent streets. This same locality attracted the attention of Norwich City Council officers, who even before the Second World War were hatching their plans to redevelop it.

An aerial photo taken in 1937 for the council (see Figure 32) neatly covers the grid of streets in question, and this has been used as the basis of our drawing showing the street layout and key locations (Figure 3). By this time the Kerrison empire encompassed both sides of Chapel Street and the adjacent roads including Salford Street and Manchester Street. Dodger's also owned houses nearby, such as at Globe Street where one property was said to be completely filled with old broken beer crates waiting for conversion into kindling.

Figure 32 Eastward aerial view of the Vauxhall Street area in 1937. The wood piles are visible left of centre with Percy's motorcycle combination parked in Chapel Street. See also Figure 3 for street labels.

Figure 33 Dodger's rubber stamp from the 1930s, often used to mark song sheets as they were sold

An Aladdin's cave

By 1935, the cycle shop had already become well known as an Aladdin's cave of parts and accessories, as well as radios, batteries (that is, accumulators which could be recharged) and gramophone records (Figure 33).

A letter to the *Evening News* (in 1994) recalled one person's visits to the shop in the 1930s:

When I was about 10 years old I used to hire his bikes and then they were just fourpence an hour. Fairy cycles, all sorts of bikes he had, and there was a big notice outside on the wall saying: 'Here's the man that won't refuse; To mend all kinds of inner tubes; His prices are small; His work is good; He only charges you what he should.'

The wood pile

There were by this time two huge accumulations of stored wood on the south side of the street, in the former garden areas in front of both No. 15 and No. 15a Chapel Street, on both sides of the Salford Street junction.[21] The first pile reached right up to the third storey – and this eventually required the use of a very long single-stage ladder, itself a landmark leaning there for at least two decades (Figure 34). Clearly these wood heaps were a fire risk, but apparently there was never a major incident. It is said Percy was particularly vigilant every year on Guy Fawkes Night to ensure no stray rocket landed on the pile!

Another alleged issue was the obstruction of highway caused by the piles of wood, hand barrows, cycles and various other items, leading to intermittent complaints from both the City Council and the police. Several orders and summonses were received from

---

21   'No. 15a Chapel Street' was technically part of No. 16 Salford Street.

Figure 34 Fulcher's coal delivery lorry outside the wood pile at the Salford Street corner, late 1920s, with the tall ladder visible to the right

Norwich City Council between 1928 and 1937 to dismantle the wood pile. A formal letter in May 1935 was received from the Chief Constable threatening proceedings if 'no action is being taken' by Mr Kerrison.

Real estate

As we have seen, there was no let-up in the process of property development during the 1930s. The family embarked on further major refurbishment of the block that included No. 15 (as pictured by George Plunkett, Figure 35, with modern view Figure 36), and from the wording on a permanent sign they put up on completion (Figure 37), it seems that the Dodgers already had an inkling of the city council's intentions to allow the area to run down and then to clear it. They acquired another corner shop at 8 Chapel Street on the opposite side a little farther to the west, for use as their 'cycle showroom'. Their more secure 'cycle store' was a former dwelling at 13 Manchester Street, and this usually contained numerous new bikes in their paper wrappings.

Figure 35 Nos 7 to 15
Chapel Street after
renovation, pictured in
1938

Figure 36 The same
viewpoint as Figure 35
photographed
79 years later

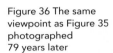

Life in the street in the years running up to the Second World War is
vividly recalled by Emily's son Ronnie
Green:

*I remember Percy sawing wood under
the huge wood pile at Chapel Street, using a circular saw driven by
a petrol engine. This was dangerous because the wood sometimes
included old joists with nails that snagged the saw. I also heard later
that he had once caught his apron-strings in the saw but luckily they
had broken before he was pulled onto it. He threw shortened sections
of timber across to the opposite side of Salford Street to where my
mother Emily (his sister) would be sitting on a large log next to a*

Figure 37 Sign
put up on 11
Chapel Street
by Percy after
the renovation
work, 1938

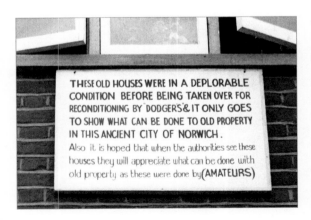

THESE OLD HOUSES WERE IN A DEPLORABLE
CONDITION BEFORE BEING TAKEN OVER FOR
RECONDITIONING BY DODGERS & IT ONLY GOES
TO SHOW WHAT CAN BE DONE TO OLD PROPERTY
IN THIS ANCIENT CITY OF NORWICH.
Also it is hoped that when the authorities see these
houses they will appreciate what can be done with
old property as these were done by (AMATEURS)

chopping block, next to another wood pile. She chopped the wood into kindling to earn 6d an hour. My job at the age of 5 or 6 was to pick up the bits that had not reached the gap where my mother was working, while dodging the next bit being thrown.

The larger woodpile often reached to the top window of the three-storey block of the terraced houses on the west side of the Salford Street junction. On a number of occasions Percy and Freddie received notices from Norwich City Council ordering them to remove, or at least lower, the wood pile. However, nobody living locally was complaining as they were able to buy kindling at 2d a bundle and everyone had an open fire at home.

As a young boy I also had to unravel rope in lengths of about 16 inches and make the single strands of string in order to bundle the wood. It was rough on my little fingers, but as there was plenty of old used rope around at that time and it saved Dodger on buying string. I recall a gadget shaped like two upturned horseshoes where the kindling was placed, then the rope strands were passed under this to tie up the bundles. I did this at No. 15 Chapel Street. No one actually lived there, and I had to go through a 'tunnel' of wood under the large wood pile to reach the front door, which was never shut. On the right hand side of this wood pile was a very tall wooden ladder reaching about ten rungs higher than the three-storey terrace.

One story goes that Percy was at the Corn Hall in Exchange Street opposite Thorns, where Jarrolds now is, and he purchased the ladder. A chap told Percy he'd get this ladder back to Chapel Street for the agreed sum of 2/6 (half a crown). With a ladder that long, an accident was bound to happen. On getting it all the way back to Chapel Street the man asked Percy Dodger for an extra half a crown – having by then put a shop window in and also knocked someone off his bike. Needless to say Percy refused to pay, having already agreed the price.

The business made much use of flat rail barrows, and Dodger had a few of these for hire. These had wooden wheels and shafts like a cart, except you were the horse. They were often used in the 1920s and 1930s to sell things from on the street, like vegetables or winkles, or by the rag and bone man. Another use was when making a moonlight flit. That happens when someone owes so much rent, they pile what little they have on the barrow chiefly at night and quickly move elsewhere. There's an old music hall song about it ...

5

Wartime and aftermath

The late 1930s in Britain had witnessed a mixture of social unrest following the Depression, celebrations at the time of the coronation, then uncertainty about the developments in Europe. After a nervous period of preparation for war which included the local delivery of gas masks and air raid shelters for the poorer households, the Declaration came in 1939.

In time, Freddie went away into the air force (based at RAF Topcliffe near Thirsk). Percy joined the Norfolk Home Guard ('C' Company 16th Battalion). Elsie remembered him blacking his face, putting netting with twigs and leaves over his steel helmet and going on night exercises. Although they trained with broom handles as dummy rifles, on one occasion they had real hand grenades in a trench. His platoon headquarters was 2 miles away, but he missed Sunday parade only once.[22] Percy was also an Air Raid Precautions warden. There was a siren nearby and an ARP post at Salford Street opposite the wood piles. It was mainly local shopkeepers who were on the wardens' rota.

In the event, this area of Norwich suffered particularly badly from bomb damage, probably because of its proximity to Caley's factory at Chapelfield, which was a visible target. A single large bomb wiped out the Vauxhall Tavern in February 1941, and the following year a number of homes in the Chapel Street area (at Union Street, Manchester Street, Globe Street and Salford Street) were severely damaged during the massive raids at the end of April (Figure 38). Some of the city council's objectives had been achieved for them in terms of building clearance, but there had of course been a regrettable loss of life.

Ronnie Green was only 5 when the war started, but has some vivid childhood memories of the time:

Rubber balls for play were not available (all the rubber was used for the war effort) so Dodger was always asked for old cycle inner tubes which could be cut up into elastic bands, then stretched criss-cross fashion over screwed-up paper, making a good ball to play cricket or rounders. Inner tubes also had ideal rubber for catapults. Some inner

---

22 On disbandment in 1944, Percy wrote a letter asking to retain his uniform (notably the boots) after members of the Home Guard had been ordered to return it or risk police proceedings.

Figure 38 Bomb damage on the east side of Manchester Street after a 1942 air raid

tubes were patched up and used while swimming in Wensum Park and Earlham Park – the only places we could go.

The first taste locally of the war was 1941 when the Vauxhall Tavern got a direct hit – we saw just a pile of bricks and wood, nothing standing taller than my young friend Pip Gedge and myself, aged 8. Later I was told that the local milkman Mr Richardson who lived opposite the tavern had got his milk cart ready in Vauxhall Street and he'd gone back down his cellar for something just as this bomb dropped. It was not an ordinary bomb, but came down on a parachute to ensure the nose landed first. It was assumed that he had been blown to kingdom come, but the cellar had slammed shut and it knocked him out. What with the commotion it wasn't until noon some seven hours later, tapping was heard, and he was found alive.

When the war started my father Reggie Green, having been in the Territorials and trained in the nearby Drill Hall, was soon called up to be a NCO Corporal. My mum Emily worried about him, but I showed her my atlas and pointed out all the red bits, i.e. those indicating the British Commonwealth. I never doubted the result of the war or that we would win.

My Granny Kerrison was often alone when the siren went, with Freddie in the Air Force, Percy in the Home Guard and Elsie doing deliveries. As we lived in the next street, my job was to run the two streets and tell Nanny the siren had gone off because she was deaf. Mother said 'Hurry back, so that I'll know you are safe.' I was never

*afraid, more intent on getting the threepenny bit my Gran always had
for me – I waited for that before running back home.*

*I remember the morning of the bombing, the Blitz, that first of two
nights in late April 1942, getting out into the street (Salford Street)
looking to my left across Globe Street. All I could see was the backs
of the houses in the next street, it was all just rubble. A young lady
like an angel to the local youngsters had lived there – she ran a little
Sunday school, and a bun and lemonade was always waiting for you.
The place was now all gone. So many died there that they were all
buried together in two long rows at the cemetery off Guardian Road.
You go there and see the names and ages of some, that's if you've got
the guts or no heart at all. Including a babe in arms three months
old ...*

*To get one's bearings as to where Chapel Street was, there's a
building there now (2017) called Bishop Herbert House, at Globe
Place. Next to it is an old sycamore tree – this stood in the front
garden of our house at no. 24 Salford Street in 1942, a terrace row
of four, the pub William IV being next door. It would be sad for me
to see the demise of that old tree. There was a direct hit opposite on
the houses across the road in the Blitz of April 1942, and that tree
may have helped save my family's lives as our house was not flattened.
As it was, all our front, middle and back doors were blown off their
hinges and landed up beyond our Anderson shelter in the back yard,
the shelter door being no more than 6 feet from the back door. Our
next door neighbours at no. 22 had a shelter out front underground –
I'm not sure what happened to them.*

*I was told that Woolworths was bombed. Straight away I was on
my way there, thinking maybe I could get my sisters (aged 6 and 4)
some dollies, a little lad of eight. It was chaos, all ARP wardens,
police and grown-ups you didn't know telling you to go back home.*

*Getting over Chapelfield was fairly easy, but along Theatre Street
was difficult with all the rubble, yet there was no longer anyone
worrying about a little boy, all too busy or stunned by the sight of their
city. Woolworths had once been a wondrous place for a youngster,
but now it was nothing (I'm upset just recalling this), no colours
other than blacks and greys, and not a remnant of anything, clothes
or toys.*

*I found myself in Bethel Street and couldn't get back via Little
Bethel Street which was blocked. I got into the Bethel Hospital garden
and tried climbing out over the wall, but was suddenly caught and
held by an ARP warden. He carried me round his shoulders quite
some way across Chapelfield, then told me off, kicked me up the
backside and told me to go home. I remember nothing more except
getting home. Mum was in the street, and I hadn't until then noticed
our front, middle and back doors were no more, and all our windows*

were smashed. Mother said 'You're going to be evacuated.' I thought
that meant I would be having a needle stuck in me ...
    I cannot recall any more of that day. I do know we went to
Wymondham late that afternoon, but I cannot remember the journey.
I must have been in shock as an 8 year old, but what I've just written
I'll never forget. I recall we'd just got a really fluffy kitten, but we
never found it – it liked sitting by the front window – all of 75 years
ago.

Throughout the war and in the years directly afterwards the
solid fuel sales continued, and the cycle side of the business
remained an important source of income as things slowly recovered. The register detailing bicycle hires for 1944 recorded 350
individual hires for the month of August alone, bikes typically
being borrowed for between two and six hours, at 6d to 1s per
hour depending on the type of bike (see Figure 39). Motorised
means of transport were however on the rise. Percy remained
keen on his motorcycles and rarely drove a car, but Freddie
bought a truck soon after returning from the war.
    George   Henry's   widow   Eliza   Kerrison   returned   from

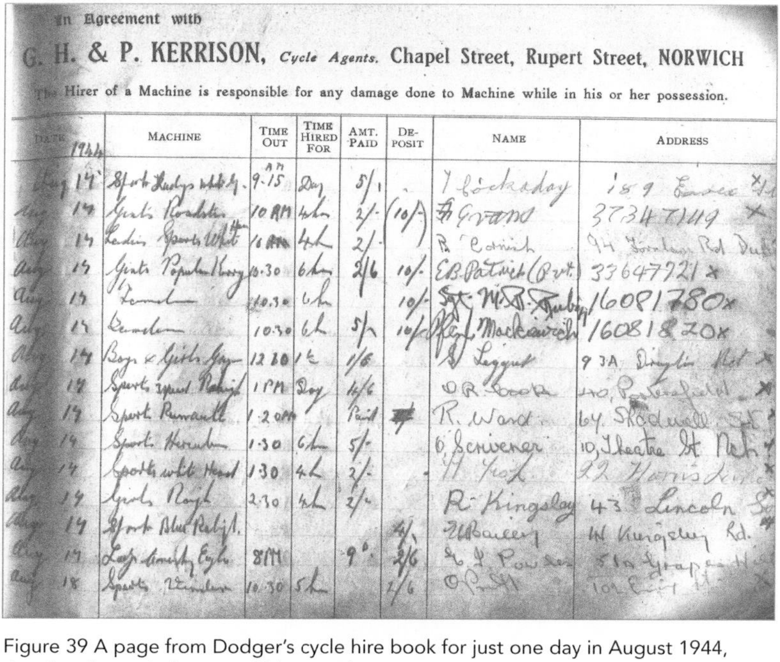

Figure 39 A page from Dodger's cycle hire book for just one day in August 1944,
showing the typical range of hirers and payments

Wymondham to Chapel Street, living at no. 13 (as recorded on her identity card) and then at no. 10. Elsie was of course also always there on site ready to help whoever needed it. Emily Green and her family returned to Norwich from Wymondham, but instead of coming to Chapel Street they settled on the Larkman estate on the west side of the city.

The Government's War Damage Commission was set up, and there was subsequent correspondence with the Kerrisons over claims for the cost of repairs, which were paid out in 1946 and 1947. Percy renewed the fire insurance cover for 15 Chapel Street in 1946.

A writer to the *Eastern Evening News* later recalled his visits to Dodger's in those post-war years: *'I remember Dodger for his ability to supply any wants during and after the war. He could always find the odd bit of wood, metal, sheets of corrugated iron, linen props, bundles of pea sticks – searching through his Aladdin's cave. If you wanted to hire a flat barrow he had one, if the baby's pram had lost a tyre there was no trouble to fit a replacement.'* He also remembered old ladies popping into the shop to buy a tin of coal just so they could have a fire that night. Those living in digs rarely had anywhere to store coal in any quantity.

Also in the years following the war, the shop at Chapel Street started to be visited regularly by American servicemen looking to buy or hire quaint English bicycles as a practical means of transport on and off their bases in East Anglia. Elsie remembered an American named Michael Moses who used to buy batches of Dodger's cycles to re-sell at the base, and the Jeep that was used to collect them. For more local excursions in the city, the bike hire charge for the Americans was 1s an hour.

Doreen remembers once throwing snowballs at visiting servicemen from the upstairs window of her home at 10 Chapel Street. Some of the transatlantic visitors had not actually seen bicycles (or snow) before, and the discovery of Dodger's collection of vintage penny farthings and other novelty bicycles was a source of great interest and amusement.

Ronnie Green remembers with a smile the reaction of the Americans: *'They didn't know what to make of it. They were like children. We had some fun with them.'*

6

The publicity machine, a starring role, a Royal Commission

Percy re-brands the business

We have already noted how Old Dodger had a flair for promotion of his business through display boards with words and pictures. While Percy remained in George Henry's shadow up until his father's death, the turmoil of the Second World War limited the opportunities for his own PR talents to emerge until the early 1950s.

Looking through successive entries in *Kelly's Directory* for the post-war years, we see the Chapel Street business continuing to be listed throughout the 1930s and 1940s as 'Kerrison G H & P, cycle agents and coal merchants', and that was what was printed on their sales tags (Figure 40). However, the business was already known informally before the war as Dodger's, and appeared as such on advertising signs in photographs taken outside the Chapel Street shop in 1938.

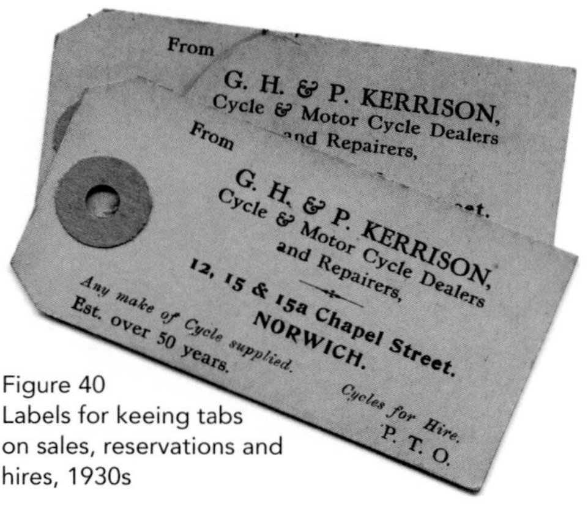

In the early 1950s a new 'official' branding appears in *Kelly's*, with the listing shown as '**DODGERS** (G H & P Kerrison)' with the use of bold capitals.[23] It seems that a conscious

Figure 40
Labels for keeing tabs on sales, reservations and hires, 1930s

___

23 Other specific addresses in Manchester Street and Salford Street also appeared

decision was made around 1951 to capitalise on the Dodger name and put it prominently on the shop, as well as on increasing amounts of printed publicity material in the form of hand bills and posters (see Appendix I), even pencils with the name on.

Aside from the intrinsic Kerrison flair for publicity and photographs, Percy seems to have been interested from this time in domestic cine films, with the increasing availability of home cameras, of which he came to acquire a collection.

A cavalcade of old cycles

By the early 1950s Percy and Freddie had accumulated a sizeable collection of antique bicycles. Some may have been machines taken in by Old Dodger during his early trading years, but these were supplemented by judicious buying at auctions – and also made possible by having sufficient indoor space to store them.

We know Percy was in touch as early as 1949 with an antique bicycle expert in Romford, researching the history of some of the older machines. As a result of the growing interest from visitors, he began to see an opportunity to use these for publicity purposes, and no Dodger was going to miss that trick.

Not long afterwards came the founding of the Dodgers Penny

in the annual listing alongside Chapel Street, remaining until the Dodger's' relocation in the late 1950s.

Figure 41 Dodgers Penny Farthing Cycling Club members, photographed in the late 1950s with Union Street in the background

Figure 42 The intrepid five penny farthing riders at Agricultural Hall en route to Great Yarmouth in September 1951. Freddie is on the left, and the hidden rider is Arthur Pestell.

Farthing Cycling Club, otherwise known as the Olde Tyme Cycling Club. This comprised a core group recruited from family members, friends and neighbours, who took to riding through the city (and sometimes farther afield) on a remarkable collection of original penny farthings (Figure 41), alongside other unusual machines that included a wooden bone-shaker, various tricycles and soon even a bedstead fitted with wheels and pedals.

In September 1951 five well-maintained penny farthings were given a run from Norwich to Great Yarmouth, to commemorate the 60th anniversary of a local cycling club (Figure 42). The journey was completed in 2 hours 35 minutes. The riders were Fred Kerrison, John Sutton, Len and Ray Stubbs, and their customary leader Arthur Pestell, a baker in Rupert Street.[24] In 1951 a series of 'official' club runs were publicised in successive box adverts in the *Evening News* (Figure 43).

You can imagine how the collection of peculiar old bikes continued to delight the American visitors (Figure 44). The Olde Tyme Cycle Club played a part in the Norwich Festival celebrations of 1951, and before long a deal had been done with local cinemas for the club to ride poster-bedecked through the city centre, the riders in fancy dress, to advertise the latest screen

---

24 The Pestells were long-standing friends, and the family used to spend long holidays in the Kerrisons' caravan on the coast at Walcott.

**DODGER'S PENNY-FARTHING
CYCLING CLUB
CLUB RUN**
Norwich to Mulbarton, return via
East Carleton. Starting point Norfolk
and Norwich Hospital.
11 a.m., SUNDAY, SEPT. 23rd, 1951
Weather Permitting

Figure 43 Box advert in the
Evening News advertising one of
several official club runs

Figure 44 A visit of American
servicemen to the showroom,
early 1950s, with Freddie on the
right

offerings, particularly films which featured bicycles. It was an
opportunity to promote not only the latest movies, but also
Dodger's cycle services – and to have some fun, after a long
period of austerity.

Local cinemas taking part included the Odeon in Botolph
Street, the Carlton in All Saints Green, and the Norvic and
Regent cinemas on Prince of Wales Road. Examples of films ad-
vertised in this way in the 1950s included *Texans Never Cry,
Ten Tall Men, Four Faces West, Cave of Outlaws, Isn't Life
Wonderful, Glad Tidings, Genevieve, Value for Money,* and
Smiley Gets a Raleigh (Figures 45 and 46).

This 'cycle cavalcade' attracted the attention of organisers of
local galas and charity fetes who were keen to have the partic-
ipation of the riders and their vintage machines. The cavalcade
appeared at the BLESMA (British Limbless Ex-Service Men's
Association) summer fetes held at Carrow Abbey from the early
1950s (Figure 47), the Norwich Festival in 1951, the Coronation
Carnival in June 1953 at Eaton Park,[25] the annual Wymondham

25 It is ironic that the attendance of the cycle cavalcade was expressly sought by city
   council officials just as their colleagues were stepping up moves to compulsorily
   purchase Dodger's premises, as described in the next chapter.

Figure 45 Movies featuring bicycles (early product placement) were an ideal opportunity for Dodger's

Figure 46 Members of the cycle cavalcade promoting the 1956 film *Smiley* in Gentleman's Walk, with Percy and Elsie riding the Olympia trike and Ivan (Freddie's son) behind on a Bantam bicycle

Figure 47 Ticket for the 1953 fete organised by BLESMA

Figure 48 A selection of decorated machines and their riders outside the showroom at 8 Chapel Street, celebrating the 1953 coronation. To the right is Manchester Street, with an Anderson shelter visible.

Carnival Fayre held on King's Head Meadow in the mid-1950s and numerous other galas. For taking part in the Coronation Carnival (Figures 48 and 49), the Kerrisons received a letter from Barclay's Bank thanking them for 'a jolly good show'.

The antique bikes also appeared in exhibitions in Blackfriars Hall, Norwich (Figure 50) and were loaned out for theatre shows

Figure 49 Percy in outfit with the Kangaroo bike, probably 1953

Figure 50 Some of Dodger's cycle collection on display in Blackfriar's Hall for Road Safety Exhibition in 1952

(such as for the Peggy Carr School of Dancing in 1951) and in later years for TV productions including Anglia Television's *About Anglia* magazine programme, and the films *Who killed Santa Claus?* and *The Black Tower.*

The high point for the Old Tyme Cycle Club was when Pathé

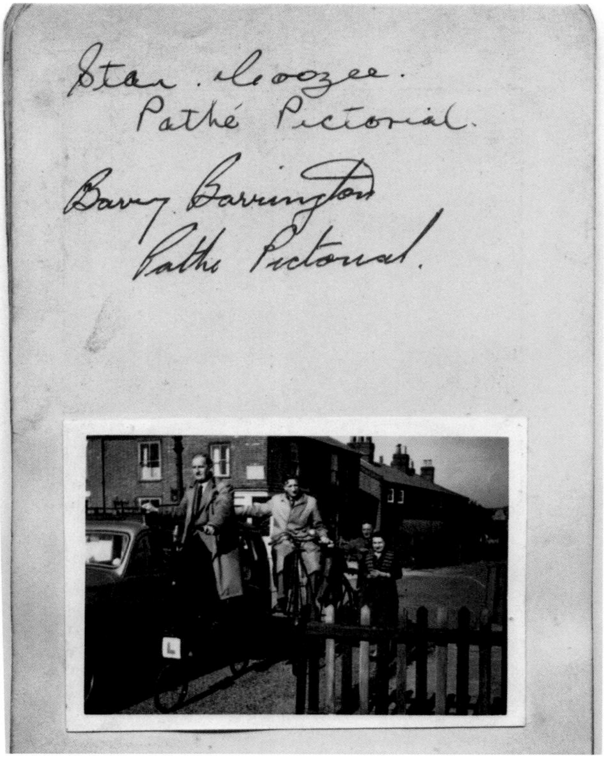

Figure 51 Page from the Dodger autograph book signed by the Pathé cameramen during their visit in October 1952, with a snap of the vehicle from which the elevated views on the cover of this book were filmed

Figure 52 Between Freddie and Percy, a sign promoting the Pathe film on the rear of Freddie's lorry

Pictorial got in touch in 1952 to say it wanted to make a short newsreel film of their activities for showing in the cinemas. Fame indeed. Pathé's film crew Stan Goozee and Barry Barrington arrived on 5 October in a car specially equipped for filming from a tripod on its roof (Figure 51). It was a challenge for Dodger to find the 25 or so people needed to ride all the bikes to include tandem passengers on the day, but the film was successfully shot at Chapel Street, Rupert Street and Newmarket Road and it was shown across the country shortly afterwards backed by the characteristic clichéd newsreel commentary.[26] It was a great source of pride for the Dodgers, and of course was milked for local promotion (Figure 52).

Unsurprisingly, almost all of the cyclists that day were male, but some of the women (including Elsie) took part as passengers on vintage tricycles. A writer to the *Evening News* in 1995 recalled visiting the shop that day: '*Pathé News were coming to film and he asked us to ride his old bikes for the camera. I can remember riding around on a tandem with a young lady at the front. A week or so later I went to the pictures and saw myself on the news.*'

Somehow the bikes even featured in cartoons in two early editions of the boy's adventure comic *Lion*, in 1952 (see Figure 53).

---

26   Hand-coloured stillstills from the film have been used on the cover of this book.

The hobby of P. Kerrison, an Englishman, is to collect ancient bikes. When this model is taken for an airing, the driver often wears a top hat and false beard.

Figure 53 Dodger's tandem trike featured in cartoon in *Lion* comic, 1952

The bedstead bike

Featured in the Pathé film was a unique creation, the bedstead bike. This was put together in 1951, and was probably Percy's idea. It was literally a large iron head-end of an old bed frame fitted with handle-bars, pedals and wheels (Figure 54).

Ronnie Green was away in the army at the time the film was made, but claims to have ridden on all the antique cycles in the collection. He also rode the bedstead, and has this hair-raising account:

Percy Dodger put together the bedstead bike, and Jimmy Clarke did the welding. It stood leaning up against a concrete wall of the three-storey terrace. The wall itself Percy had built. He did this first by a erecting a double wall of planks 6 inches apart then putting cement in between, throwing in some old cycle frames and forks, then filling the gaps with concrete.

Once the cement had set, he took away the planks and there you have your wall.

I climbed onto the wall and lowered myself on the bike. Percy said,

Figure 54 The bedstead bike is well displayed in this view, as ridden by Arthur Pestell alongside Freddie Kerrison on the Ariel Ordinary, in 1953

'You'll break your neck, wait till Freddie gets home.' I was about 17 then. This contraption had racing drop handlebars turned upwards and big brass knobs on each end – after all it was the head-end of an old bed frame.

I'd done idiotic things before – and later in life I was to climb the tallest chimney in West Germany. Well, I rode away from the wall and all seemed OK, past the big woodpile from where I started – this part of the street didn't have a path. Once I got across Salford Street to Union Street, there was a path, which proved my downfall. Suddenly I was pedalling rather faster, and realised the chain was off. I had enough momentum to reach a fence but the path edge was approaching. I cocked my leg to get off as for a conventional bike, but to my dismay the brass knob at the back was in my way being as I was only 5'2' tall. Well I did what a famous jockey of these times (Frankie Dettori) does on winning occasions, but not so gracefully. I duly hit the ground, after which the bike fell on top of me. The problem was the chain had derailed, it being so far between the crank and the back wheel which meant the whole thing swayed a bit. An iron bar was added that evening, and the chain never came off afterwards.

The next day I was again on the bedstead on the very same spot, with my young friend Peter Copping alongside me on a penny farthing. 'Hang on,' I said as we set off, 'I've got to find somewhere to get off.' I turned left into Union Street, then left again into Coach and Horses Street by the pub, and there was a high double gate. This I leaned against, but it was off the latch, and to my dismay it swung open. I was quickly heading down onto a shingle path on my side followed by the bedstead onto my other side.

The cyclists most photographed on the bedstead were Freddie (Dodger) Kerrison and Arthur Pestell, the local baker, with Arthur's grandchildren often accompanying him on a three wheeler tandem.

I've mentioned having done idiotic things, and the old adage is true: one never learns. Once again, I was atop the bedstead bike. Most of the other regular riders sensibly preferred to ride penny farthings. And what a sight – we all were going along Unthank Road that time, six or seven of us, although I was well behind at the back. The plan was to turn right into Christchurch Road before Colman Road, pass three streets then turn left through to Colman Road and back to Unthank. Well, being behind, I turned left at the first street off Christchurch Road as a short cut to get in front of the others and get to the Colman Road traffic lights before the others. To my horror the lights turned red, but luckily a van pulled up just in the right place for me to lean against. I looked round to see where the lads were just as the lights went green and the van pulled away. Down I went for the third time off the bedstead.

More of Ronnie's cycling adventures can be found in Appendix IV.

Wordsmiths

A notable feature of the Dodgers' publicity throughout the years was the use of words, both painted on signboards (on buildings, bikes and other vehicles) and printed on handbills. These were often arranged into rhyme, and although some examples must have been penned by Old Dodger himself, we know others were written by family

Figure 55 Adam Onikoyi posing on a penny farthing at the Chapel Street/Manchester Street junction during his visit in 1951

members including Ronnie's sister June, and by a self-styled poet named William Earl (known as Norfolk Bill).[27]

In Appendix I is a collection of Dodger rhymes (of variable poetic quality) which give a flavour of how this all added to the publicity.

By 1952, Elsie was able to tell a visiting reporter (*Eastern Evening News*, 2 September) that 'We have made friends all over the country and abroad.' To support this claim, she proffered the Dodger autograph book, which in the space of two months had collected signatures and photographs from customers literally 'all over the place'.

The idea of the autograph book originated in 1951 when Mr Adam Onikoyi, the Deputy Town Clerk of Lagos, Nigeria, was staying in Norwich and visited the shop (Figure 55). The Kerrisons learned of his status by chance, and made sure of obtaining his autograph when he called a second time. Subsequently they encouraged all their customers to pose with their vintage cycles, and made sure no celebrities passed unrecognised. The

27 William Earl was an ex-soldier who had originally enlisted in the Norfolk Militia in 1882, but was finally demobilised in 1919 because of what would today be called post traumatic stress disorder.

surviving autograph book records the Pathé film makers, and numerous visitors from Germany, France, Netherlands, Africa, America, Australia and other countries.

This sort of publicity became a useful weapon once the rumblings of city council compulsory purchase started, as described in the next chapter.

Royal commission

The hiring-out of bicycles had for many years been a key part of the business, and it could be said this was both profitable for Dodgers and also a socially beneficial thing for the local community. However, the firm's reputation for providing bikes for hire spread far beyond the city.

A television documentary on the Queen Mother shows the Royal Family cycling at Sandringham (King George VI with Princesses Elizabeth and Margaret), and these were bicycles supplied by Dodger.

Percy proudly kept a framed letter from Buckingham Palace

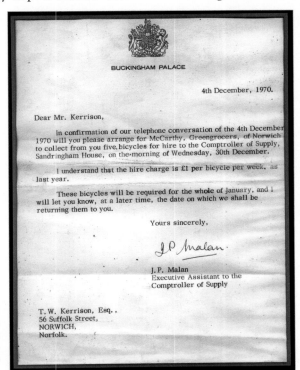

BUCKINGHAM PALACE

4th December, 1970.

Dear Mr. Kerrison,

In confirmation of our telephone conversation of the 4th December 1970 will you please arrange for McCarthy, Greengrocers, of Norwich to collect from you five bicycles for hire to the Comptroller of Supply, Sandringham House, on the morning of Wednesday, 30th December.

I understand that the hire charge is £1 per bicycle per week, as last year.

These bicycles will be required for the whole of January, and I will let you know, at a later time, the date on which we shall be returning them to you.

Yours sincerely,

J.P. Malan

J. P. Malan
Executive Assistant to the
Comptroller of Supply

T. W. Kerrison, Esq.,
56 Suffolk Street,
NORWICH,
Norfolk.

Figure 56 Framed letter confirming the arrangements for a royal commission for cycle hire relating to the hiring of bicycles from Dodger's for Sandringham a little later on (Figure 56). Whether or not he was offered the chance of using the royal crest, he never, so far as we know, exploited this most sought-after opportunity for publicity.

7

Compulsory purchase, the empire dismantled

Gathering clouds

The post-war years of the 1950s in Britain were a time of austerity, gradually giving way to optimism for the future. For Dodger's the decade had begun with the emergence of the Old Tyme Cycle Club, but those jolly antics were soon being played out against a background of gathering disquiet arising from the city council's stated intention to clear and redevelop the Union Place area of which Chapel Street was the centre.

In time this intensified into an all-out battle over the territory that Dodger's had not only occupied for more than half a century, but over most of the real estate that had been accumulated by the dynasty in the meantime.

Norwich City Council had for a number of years set its mind to substantially improve large areas of the city through slum clearance. This was implemented during the 1930s – but hitherto it had been done in the older areas within the city centre (such as the Bull Close area). After publication of the bold City of Norwich Plan of 1945, the policy was extended to include areas of poorer-quality housing outside the urban core, including the Vauxhall Street area which had suffered so badly from enemy action.

Norwich City Council has often been commended on the strength of its housing policies, which certainly improved the living conditions of countless tenants. However, when you have built or repaired your own home and are then told it is to be acquired and flattened, it becomes personal. To the extended family of Dodgers, it felt like they were being picked on. Since the 1930s they had shrugged off repeated civic complaints over the woodpile, but it now seemed to them a resentful corporation was intent on punishing them for their local popularity and Dodger's success in building a local property empire.

Resistance

On receiving official notification of the first compulsory purchase order in 1952, Percy's reaction was to write to the advice page of the *News of the World*.[28] He received a less than encouraging reply about the chances of avoiding eventual eviction, and was advised to appoint a lawyer. As the result of numerous property purchases, Dodger's already had one – Daynes Chittock of Opie Street.

Then followed a long war of communications, stand-offs and committee decisions which lasted throughout the 1950s. Many letters were sent out by the Kerrisons, often drafted in Percy's hand and typed up by his niece June or by lawyers. They also took many photographs in an attempt to demonstrate that their properties were in better condition than was being claimed (indeed better than the council's own stock), and to support the view of local people that it was wanton destruction of good homes that was being planned.

The family's approach (at least as it was seen from their side) was summarised in a letter Elsie drafted to the *Eastern Evening News*:

Although the general public are with us, some of them might appear to be under the delusion that we are fighting the Norwich corporation. Nothing could be further from the truth.

Since 1952 we and our solicitor have made every endeavour to co-operate with the council to come to an agreeable solution. When we knew of the council's decision to redevelop the Vauxhall Street area, we had plans drawn up for a new house, shop and business premises, to be developed on our main site, thereby relinquishing the rest of our properties and keeping to one site. Failing this we suggested an alternative site, freehold for freehold, next to Thomas Gill's – this was and is vacant land.[29] Our suggestion was refused.

When we knew of T. Gill's intention to move, our solicitor tried for that site, this also was refused us. Finally we asked for a portion of that land – far less than the land we now own, but sufficient for us to carry on business in the neighbourhood without unnecessary detriment to us and our customers. All we wanted was a fair exchange of land. The Norwich corporation has done this for other firms in the city. Why not us?

We approached Councillor Rix, the representative for our ward and obtained a meeting with three leading officials in Councillor Rix's presence. We discussed our case with them, and showed them the plans we had prepared in 1952. We also showed them T. Gill's mill that has stood vacant for nearly 4 years, and the site we would be prepared to take. We told them our case could have been settled

28 The Chapel Street area was subject to two compulsory purchase orders, of 1952 and 1955, both subordinate to the County Borough of Norwich Declaratory Order of 1948.

29 This building firm previously had premises in Rupert Street.

amicably five years ago. At the end of the discussion we had hopes that at last we would get fair and just treatment.

The next thing we knew, an eviction order was served and it was clear it had already been agreed. An Independent councillor told us that some members of the council were not happy about it. The rest the public know.

Even while we are doing our best to clear our main site, we are still threatened with eviction, not only the site we are engaged in clearing but the rest of our business premises and our own homes, for all members of the family live in close proximity to the business. It is unfortunate also that the council ripped up a road adjoining our property, for it had been agreed under seal between the local officials, our solicitors and two barristers that this was not to be done.

We hope that it is now clear that far from fighting Norwich corporation, we are indeed being oppressed and that they are the oppressors.

In another letter to the press, Elsie describes the stress all this was causing them:

... we have not unnaturally been very concerned with our business premises and our future livelihood. I wonder if the councillors of this city realise the worry and anxiety they are causing the families of this firm.

At every stage, there were orders to fight, advice to be sought and misunderstandings to correct. There were claims and counter-claims of damp and substandard buildings. The family were on the one hand being ordered to quit, and on the other not being offered suitable alternative freehold or even leasehold premises, either to live in or from which to run their business. When it came later to being given property valuations for compulsory purchase (bearing in mind the number of properties they had acquired),[30] they were understandably upset about the rock-bottom prices offered, seeing this as proof of the council's policy to 'rob the Dodgers'.

Along the way the Dodgers' plight gained local support in the *Evening News*, and their own publicity machine was also harnessed, leading to the sight of the Olde Tyme Cycle Club

---

30 This was partly because of a change in the compulsory purchase legislation in
1955–56. The District Valuer frequently was required only to compute a value
for the land, ignoring the house which was to be demolished. For example, a
nine-roomed tenanted house, garage and garden in Coach and Horses Street
bought by Freddie in 1943 for £300 was compulsorily purchased for £90 in
1958, working out at 6/- a square yard. What was particularly galling to the
family was that part of it was subsequently resold by the council to a brewery for
a car park, allegedly at a considerable profit.

Figure 57 The Penny Farthing Club is at it again,
publicising a petition against eviction of the Dodgers,
pictured at Dereham Road in 1952

riding through the city gathering signatures on a public petition
in protest at the eviction and proposed clearance (Figures 57 and
58). Elsie and Percy continued to be in contact with national
newspapers, seeking both advice and publicity.

For the council's part, it must have been inconvenient and awkward being up against a doughty family who commanded such
a level of local popular support. Towards the end of the six-year
battle, a letter was sent in March 1958 by Bernard Storey (Town
Clerk) to Dodger's' solicitor which could not conceal the extreme
levels of exasperation that had been reached at City Hall.

*… I have endeavoured on many occasions to make it plain to your
clients that possession of their properties is urgently needed, and
while it has been possible from time to time since then to make
certain limited concessions, the redevelopment of the area cannot be
postponed any longer…*

Figure 58 Elsie
collecting
signatures for
the petition,
outside the
Regal cinema
in Dereham
Road

*... Should I be obliged to call upon the Sheriff to deliver posses-
sion, the cost of the service and issue of the warrant will, under the
provisions of Section 91 of the Land Clauses Act 1845, fall upon
them...*

*The Housing Manager informs me he has made absolutely no
progress with your clients over the question of alternative living
accommodation...*

He went on perhaps mischievously to suggest that Percy and
Elsie were themselves in dispute as to the suitability of a house
they were being offered at 27 Victoria Street.

Eliza passes away

Midway through this tortuous series of battles, Old Dodger's
ageing widow Eliza passed away in 1955. She was the mother
to those at the forefront of the fight, but mercifully she at least
never had to face being evicted from her home.

Her personal estate included freehold properties at 7–11
Chapel Street, 12 Globe Street, 26 Manchester Street, and
'Sunnyside' at Wymondham. Contrary to the normal practice,
those acting for the family sought to value the Norwich properties as high as possible for probate purposes, in an attempt
to maximise the amount the family might subsequently receive
from the council's compulsory purchase.

Defeat

In the end, by 1957, the Dodgers had to accept the bitter inevi-
tability that their original home base would be erased and that
their future accommodation would be physically separated from
their business premises. They had lost, but Elsie later insisted
that with their backs to the wall, the family put up a good fight.

Elsie owned one house and like her brothers, was paid far
less than its true value in the end. Percy was forced to come out
of his cycle shop and had to try to continue trading in another
part of the district. All the family bar Emily had lost their home,
and some went to live at Adelaide Street off Dereham Road.
Elsie and Percy purchased storage premises at Allen's Lane, off
Newmarket Road and not too far from Union Street. This was
a former military site and included a huge hangar-like shed.
Freddie sold his business to the council but they would not pay

Figure 59 The wood pile finally goes. Freddie and Walter Buttolph dismantling the pile for removal to Allens Lane, 1958

Figure 60 The same viewpoint as for Figure 59 photographed 79 years later

his price for his large stack of wood. With the help of his uncle, he loaded his lorry with the wood (Figure 59, with modern comparative view in Figure 60), and transferred what remained of his business to Allen's Lane.[31]

The necessary process of downsizing provided the 'Whiffler' column in the *Evening News* with many column-inches describing interesting items that had been turned out and put up for sale at auction, such as these from June 1958:

Mr Percy Kerrison told me that as the Corporation had compulsorily acquired his business premises he was entitled to ask them to purchase his stock and had, in fact, sold much of it to them. 'Five full furniture van loads have gone away, and a sixth is going on Saturday,' he told me. 'The Corporation is selling my stuff in the Corn Exchange auctions.'

Clearing out the accumulation of years has brought to light an astonishing lot of odds and ends. 'Dodger' showed me some of these 'antiquities'. There were horns for old-type gramophones, some in their original wrappings. There was an old-fashioned typewriter, on which the letters were on a cylinder, instead of at the end of a rod – it was actuated by keys, though. What looked to me like a pair of wooden clappers for scaring birds turned out to be an old-fashioned lemon squeezer. Old-fashioned, too, were the bulb horns Mr Kerrison showed me – not to mention some 1914 copies of The Motor Cycle, *which sold at the old-fashioned price of 1d!*

... In the Corn Hall saleroom yesterday I noticed a collection of

---

31   The resulting wood pile at Allen's Lane was later entirely destroyed by fire.

Figure 61 Percy and Freddie emptying the cycle store at Manchester Street, examining a rare Facile penny farthing

cycles and accessories for sale. Then I saw Mr 'Dodger' Kerrison among the crowd, and learned that these lots were some he was unable to store while looking for new premises to replace those compulsorily

Figure 62 Surrendering the showroom to the bailiff, with the adjacent buildings already under demolition

acquired from him by the council in the Vauxhall Street clearance area. The cycles generally fetched prices which Mr Kerrison thought reasonable, but several people got bargains. A lightweight racing frame – 'it would cost 11 guineas retail,' said Dodger – went for £3. A collection of three-speed hubs, second-hand, but in good condition, fetched around a shilling a piece. Among the lots were accessories I have not seen since my boyhood days – oil-burning cycle lamps. A box of them fetched a few shillings. Five cycle headlamps, new-looking, most of them, went for two half-crowns.

Even in the final scenes, there was prevarication and dispute over the removal of stock and the vacating of properties, right up to when the bailiffs arrived. A blow-by-blow account of their arrival at Manchester Street and discussion that ensued was printed in the Evening News on 17 April 1958, and all the new cycles had to be extracted and stacked in the street (Figure 61).

A photographer must have already been invited to witness the moment the keys were handed over to the shop two months later, the adjoining half of which had already been taken down (Figure 62), and a report found its way onto the front page of the newspaper (Figure 63). The detailed official list made later of items of stock-in-trade removed from various Kerrison premises runs to many pages.

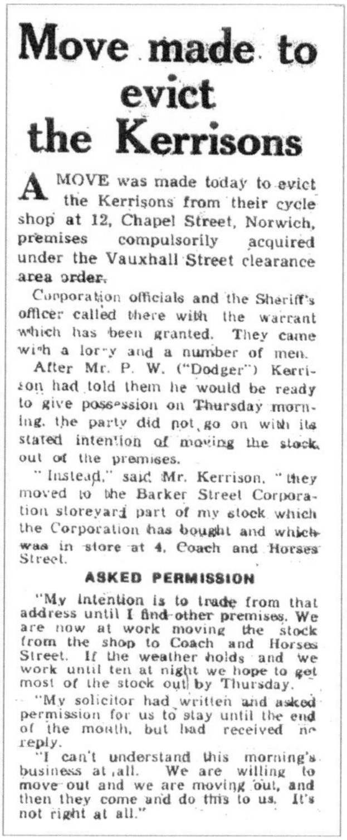

Move made to evict the Kerrisons

A MOVE was made today to evict the Kerrisons from their cycle shop at 12, Chapel Street, Norwich, premises compulsorily acquired under the Vauxhall Street clearance area order.

Corporation officials and the Sheriff's officer called there with the warrant which has been granted. They came with a lorry and a number of men.

After Mr. P. W. ("Dodger") Kerrison had told them he would be ready to give possession on Thursday morning, the party did not go on with its stated intention of moving the stock out of the premises.

"Instead," said Mr. Kerrison, "they moved to the Barker Street Corporation storeyard part of my stock which the Corporation has bought and which was in store at 4, Coach and Horses Street.

ASKED PERMISSION

"My intention is to trade from that address until I find other premises. We are now at work moving the stock from the shop to Coach and Horses Street. If the weather holds and we work until ten at night we hope to get most of the stock out by Thursday.

"My solicitor had written and asked permission for us to stay until the end of the month, but had received no reply.

"I can't understand this morning's business at all. We are willing to move out and we are moving out, and then they come and do this to us. It's not right at all."

Figure 63 Article on front page of *Eastern Evening News*, 17 June 1958

Relocations

Elsie remained with her brother Percy and helped him in his cycle business, relocated to a run-down Regency house at Pier Cottage, 4 Coach and Horses Street, and operating there for slightly less than a year (Figures 64 and 65).

Then they moved on what was former builder's premises at

Figure 64 Noel Spencer's drawing of Dodger's temporary base at Coach & Horses Street, 1959

Figure 65 A similar view of Pier Cottage, Coach & Horses Street, photographed soon before they moved out

57 Suffolk Street that Percy had bought in 1958 (Figure 66), trading from there for ten years, before finally moving into a former butcher's corner shop at 128 Cambridge Street (69 Trinity St) around 1971 (Figure 67).

Figure 66 Dodgers' premises at 57 Suffolk Street, early 1960s

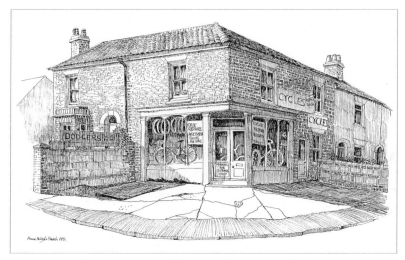

Figure 67 Anne Holgate's drawing of Dodger's final shop at 128 Cambridge Street, drawn in 1991. Can be compared with the modern view in Figure 87.

Each shop quickly became the characteristic clutter of bikes, parts, old posters and other items, always with a clock facing prominently out through the window.

Of course it was not only the Dodgers whose lives were displaced by the compulsory purchases and clearance in the Vauxhall Street area. Other long-established firms such as Gooch Builders (who had been the undertakers for Old Dodger's funeral) were forced to move away. For private residents who had to be uprooted it was particularly difficult, and some individuals, such as a Mrs Sharpe of Cross Globe Street, refused to move out to the very end, as the bailiffs and demolition men moved in.

A wasteland

The bulldozers and wrecking balls had already begun the work by the late 1950s (Figure 68), and Dodger's were continuing to trade in the midst of what had become a large demolition site (Figures 69 and 70).

Part of the block of buildings of which the cycle showroom formed a part was already removed (Figure 71) before the bailiffs visited, closely followed by the demolition men. Imagine Percy's thoughts as the premises he helped erect less than 25 years previously were torn down (Figure 72).

Many residents and businesses in the Rupert Street/Vauxhall

Figure 68 The end of an era, as the bulldozing of the Chapel Street area commences in 1958

Figure 69 View across the remains of Globe Street to the rear of 7-15 Chapel Street prior to eviction 1958–59

Figure 70 Rough road: the view up Manchester Street towards Globe Street immediately before demolition 1959

Figure 71
Hanging on:
northward
view of 10–12
Chapel Street
amidst the
demolition,
after removal
of 7–15 Chapel
Street

Figure 72 The
Royal Standard
falls: 10–12
Chapel Street
finally
succumbs,
possibly being
watched by
Percy, in 1959

Street area shared the same fate (Figures 73, 74 and 75). Two years later the clearance area extended north to Chapelfield Road, erasing the premises to which Dodger's had temporarily retreated (Figure 76).

The whole of the previously vibrant locality had become a flattened wasteland. The only two buildings spared were the

Figure 73 (across page) Composite westward view across Rupert Street, now Vauxhall Street, around 1960, with the site of the Black Eagle PH on the right. The Foreman's butcher's building still remains in 2017 as Butler's.

Figure 74 The survivor: Butler's building pictured in 2017

Figure 75 The view farther to the left from Figure 73, with Arthur Pestell's billboard visible, and the spire of Holy Trinity Church in the background

Coach & Horses public house and the Foreman's butcher's shop in Rupert Street opposite the end of Chapel Street.[32] Then followed what seemed a long period of time before the area was finally redeveloped in 1962, realising the planning dreams of the City Architect David Percival (Figures 77 and 78).

The strain of this period undoubtedly took its toll. You can

32 Formerly 26 Rupert Street, renumbered 98 Vauxhall Street, and ironically ended up as a vegetarian shop (Butler's) which still stands at the time of writing.

Figure 76 Northward
view from the Coach
& Horses, now in
Walpole Street, towards
Chapelfield Road and
The Crescent, early
1960s

From slums to smart flats in old Vauxhall Street

THE second phase of the Vauxhall Street re-development scheme in Norwich is now almost completed. The remaining flats, old people's dwellings and maisonettes will be ready for occupation by the end of next month.

Accommodation for nearly 1000 people has been provided at a cost of around £500,000, or £500 a person. More people are now living in the area than at any time since the war, although the density of population is still not so great as it was pre-war.

"The whole scheme," says the City Architect (Mr. David Percival), "has been marked by the close collaboration between my department and private architects.

Responsibilities

"No fewer than four other architects, or architectural departments, have co-operated. My responsibility has been the housing and lay-out, but Messrs. Purcell & Johnson have been responsible for Boshiers' garage, Messrs. Lacons for the re-designed Coach and Horses public-house, Messrs. Bullards for the Vauxhall Tavern, a con-temporary pub, and Messrs. Feilden & Mawson for the new veterinary premises which are being built at the

MR. DAVID PERCIVAL
ARCHITECT
corner of Chapel Field and Vauxhall Street.

When Mr. Percival came to Norwich seven years ago one of the first jobs he was given was to revise the Vauxhall Street layout because the

Town Planning Committee wished to change one or two aspects of it.

He also suggested closing Chapel Street, cutting down the traffic and making the central feature, Globe Place, a pedestrian square which can be approached from four directions.

Mr. Percival hit upon the idea of a visual connection between Chapel Field Road and the centre of the development.

Fifteen acres of land were acquired compulsorily, and of these 12½ were used for residential development. The remainder was leased, or sold for business development, reserved for the site of an Elim Church, used for building Bishop Herbert House, and for a playing field for the Bignold School.

The work has been carried out by four contractors, but nearly two-thirds of the dwellings have been built by the City Engineer's direct labour department.

At the time the development was planned the wind of change blew the financial incentives in favour of four-storey blocks. So, for the first time, a number of these were constructed, with the emphasis being on dwellings for old and single people.

All the dwellings were fitted with fires capable of burning smokeless fuel, but already there is evidence that smoke-less fuel is not being burnt by the discolouration of some chimney stacks.

Figure 77
Redevelopment of the
Vauxhall street area
underway in 1962. The
viewpoint is similar to
that in Figure 75.

Figure 78 An
article on the Vauxhall
Street scheme in the
Eastern Evening News,
23 March 1962

Figure 79 Freddie and Percy outside the Suffolk Street shop, with the hospital chimney behind and a new block of flats on Union Street in the background

Figure 80 Jenny Lind Playground, 2017, looking across Union Street at the same flats near the corner of what is now Wessex Street (previously Essex Street)

see this etched on the faces of Percy and Freddie in a photograph taken in the early 1960s outside their temporary premises in Suffolk Street (Figures 79 and 80). Elsie was also later to suffer a breakdown, perhaps caused by the prolonged trauma of it all.

Further skirmishes

Even by the 1960s, the 'hounding of the Dodgers' (as they saw it) was not over. Percy and Freddie's premises at Allen's Lane too became part of a city council improvement area, and a new compulsory purchase order duly arrived in 1968. Although they were by now living elsewhere, the brothers again felt this had to be fought, for the sake of their business. They appealed to the council not again to put them through the stress they had previously endured in being moved out of Chapel Street. There was a minor victory in 1970 when the city council decided (in a letter signed by Norwich's first city planning officer Alfie Wood) to exclude 27 and 27a Allen's Lane and a series of garages from the Arlington project.[33]

As a postscript, an *Evening News* editorial of 26 February 1965 discussing another 'improvement area' at West Pottergate regretted the heavy-handed action that had been taken by Norwich City Council during the 1950s Vauxhall Street re-development, which had 'steam-rollered small traders out of existence'. The writer suggested the council 'should try more re-alistically to help the small business people to carry on – the hive of men working on their own account, giving the community a kind of service not found elsewhere on the same terms'.

---

33 Even Adelaide Street, where Percy, Elsie and other family members now lived, was subject to city council controlling action, as was land Percy owned at West Pottergate and at the junction of Dereham Road and Heigham Road – lending weight to their sense of being hounded.

8

Dodger's later years

A plateau

The 1960s saw a period of consolidation for the business after all the disruption of removals at the end of the 1950s. The cycle shop remained for a decade based at Suffolk Street, witnessing at close hand the construction of the new maternity block on the Norfolk & Norwich Hospital site which was undergoing major expansion over the former residential streets off Union Street.[34]

Apart from the traditional trade of bike sales, repairs and accessories, there remained a healthy demand for bike hire, especially during the holiday season and from overseas visitors.

In October 1962 a letter arrived from a German customer asking 'Mr Percy' to return papers and everything accidentally left in the side-bag of a hired bicycle, by no means the only forgetful hirer depending on Dodger's kindness in returning lost property. Percy's vintage cycles also continued to be loaned for television and film productions.[35]

From time to time, Percy and Freddie put on their suits and attended cycle industry invitation visits to large factories in the Midlands, such as to the Raleigh works in 1961. A commemorative photograph shows Freddie cheerfully drinking wine, but Percy not.

An advertising bill of the time includes a bewilderingly long list of some of the items you could obtain at Suffolk Street (Figure 81). As late as 1972, Percy was still supplying paraffin from his bulk store on site, and was featured in the *Eastern Daily Press* refilling portable gas appliances during the power cuts of that year.

Suffolk Street was on borrowed time, and in June 1968 Percy had succeeded in buying a shop at 128 Cambridge Street for £3,000 from a retired butcher Mr Sadd. He transferred the retail business there a couple of years later, keeping the previous base

---

34 It was not until 2001 that the general hospital moved out to its present site at Colney.

35 An example was Anglia TV's *Weaver's Green*, a 1960s soap opera filmed in Heydon.

**Why not get it at
D O D G E R 'S**

We sell . . .

Mill Brand Ceiling White
Wallpaper Paste & Size
Methylated Spirits
Turps, Linseed Oil
Paint Brushes
Paint, Varnish & Stains
Paint Remover & Wall Plaster
Chrome & Car Cleaner
Motor Oil & Grease
Hand Soap & Razor Blades
Flints, Wicks & Gas Lighters
Electric Light Bulbs
Flex, Fuse Wire & Adapters
Fire Lighters & Pre Packed Coal
Linen Props & Posts
Pink, Blue & Golden Paraffin
Wicks & Oil Cans
Pram Wheels Repaired
New Tyres Fitted
Cycle, Torch & Transistor Batteries
DON'T FORGET . . .
WE BUY, SELL, REPAIR & HIRE CYCLES
Your Old Cycle taken in Part Exchange
All Makes Supplied
New & Second Hand
Juvenile Cycles & Tricycles.

D O D G E R 'S

57 Suffolk Street, Norwich

TEL: 22499

Figure 81 Handbill from the 1960s listing a range of goods and services available from Dodger's

for storage until it was finally demolished. The site of 57 Suffolk Street now lies beneath landscaped grass in the middle of what is now the Jenny Lind Park.

Freddie passed away in 1977, and there was Elsie and Percy left to direct the business, assisted from time to time by family

Figure 82 Percy outside the Cambridge Street shop in the late 1970s

members who worked only to their instructions. It was business as usual as Percy approached his 80s (Figure 82).

Hidden assets

Had you visited Percy 'Dodger' Kerrison at his shop on the Cambridge Street/Trinity Street corner in the 1980s, you would have encountered an eccentric old man in an old-fashioned emporium, soldiering on the way he always had, seemingly oblivious to the modern world (Figure 83). Perhaps you'd wonder how he could make it pay, with such an excess stock of bicycle bits at old-fashioned prices, occupying run-down premises with so few serious customers.

That impression was a true one, but it was only one side that you saw. You may not have been aware of the back story we

Figure 83 By the 1980s the shop was becoming a bit dilapidated, and Percy was in his 80s

Figure 84 Sunnyside at Norwich Road, Wymondham, standing empty in the 1980s

have described, the long history of a family business stretching from the end of the nineteenth century, Percy himself closely involved for most of that period. And even more hidden from view was the property empire that Dodger continued to dabble with, with a little help, into his last years.

The papers suggest Percy had been behind many of the property purchases (at auction and in other ways) from the 1920s onwards, while his father was still alive. While paperwork was never his strong point, that did not prevent him continuing to wheel and deal into his 80s. It surprising just how many properties or pieces of land Percy owned in Norwich, and it has not been possible to compile a full list (see Appendix III for those in the Chapel Street area).

Sunnyside, the house that had been bought at Wymondham in the 1930s, was still on the books in the 1980s.[36] It was on the main Norwich Road and had formerly been connected with a nearby laundry and wash house. The plot included outbuildings, an orchard and approximately 2 acres of land. It was probably originally bought for members of the Impey family who lived in the Wymondham area, but had then housed members of the Kerrison family during the Second World War. It had become vacant and dilapidated (Figure 84), and planning permission was obtained for residential redevelopment. After much prevarication, Elsie and Percy eventually sold it to a developer in 1992. The old house was dismantled and the bricks sold, and the site is now part of Oakwood Drive. 'Sunnyside' only survives today

---

36 This was always said by family members to be the house that George Henry's sons were away from Norwich bidding for at the time in 1935 he was bitten by the rat. The brothers acquired it for £200 and it was the property to which Elsie and her mother Eliza and her family were evacuated during the Blitz seven years later. A letter has since turned up in the archive showing that in fact Sunnyside was purchased by Eliza two years earlier in May 1933, in which case the brothers must have been away for some other purpose.

only as the name Ronnie Green gave to his home at Old Palace Road, Norwich.

In 1983 a substantial holding of land at Horsford owned jointly by Percy and Freddie was sold to a housing developer, and the proceeds split between them. In 1984–85 there was dealing over the plot of land Percy owned to the rear of houses near to the junction of Dereham Road and Heigham Road.[37]

A life of bicycles

What is undeniable is that Percy Dodger Kerrison remained dedicated to his life's practical work with bicycles. Perhaps he simply didn't know any other way. He worked all hours, but the opening times of the shop were becoming erratic towards the end. Even so, the nurses of the nearby hospital remained grateful customers: Percy's charges for repairs were considered reasonable, and he did an excellent job. It is probable he rather enjoyed their visits.

He remained proud and protective of his business. When another cycle shop opened nearby on Cambridge Street,[38] he promptly placed a note in his window disclaiming any connection. It was at this time that he even received letters from people sending in their CVs seeking employment in the business.

Percy also never gave up his gripes against the city council. In 1977 the *Evening News* reported how Mr Dodger Kerrison had complained about City Hall having an extra day's holiday when he wanted information about who was organising the street procession.

Every so often his past caught up with him and the media men came calling. Usually it was to take a look at the antique bikes, some of which were stacked up in his sheds at Allen's Lane. Reporter James Ruddy of the *Evening News* dressed up in Edwardian costume in September 1983 to have his picture taken climbing onto a penny farthing (Figure 85), and riding in tandem with 82-year-old Percy. Two TV programmes were made by Anglia Television for their *Bygones* series: Percy's shop

---

37 It is rumoured he may have owned a small plot of ground near Haymarket in central Norwich, the transfer of which caused a delay to the building of the new C&A store in 1969. He may also have had a share of some other businesses, such as Jack Brand's Fruiterers on Norwich market.

38 This was Specialised Cycles, the proprietor of which made a determined attempt to acquire Dodger's in 1989–90, but Percy and Elsie would not have it.

Figure 85 Reporter James Ruddy climbs on the Ariel penny farthing under Percy's supervision, September 1983

environment and his ability to tell tales of the old days must have suited the show. Elsie had initially rushed about trying to tidy the shop ahead of their arrival, but as the presenter told her, 'if we'd wanted Halfords, we'd have gone to Halfords.'

With such publicity it is perhaps unsurprising that there were burglaries: two men were convicted for theft in 1984, and a further two valuable penny farthings were stolen from the shop later in the early 1990s – never to be seen or heard of again.

To the end of the road

As late as 1986 his bikes were still in demand: the 'Gasp up Gas Hill' event organised by Friends of the Earth offered have-a-go rides on Dodger's 'wibbly-wobbly bike' for 10p a try, and his shop advert also appeared in the event programme.

In his final years when he could no longer pedal to work, he was taking a taxi daily from Adelaide Street to his cycle shop in Cambridge Street, the last resting place of the Dodger cycle business.

Percy had spent virtually all of his life working in the same small area of Norwich. He ended his days in a nursing home at Whitehall Road, not so very far away from where all the dramas of his life had occurred. He died on 5 November 1995, a day before his 94th birthday.

Reminiscences flood in

Following a piece about Percy's death by Derek James in the *Evening News* in late 1995 and a later appeal for stories by Percy's niece Joyce in 1998, local people sent in memories and tributes. Many commented on how time seemed frozen in Dodger's shop.

Stepping through the door was to step back in time, nothing seemed to have changed for decades. Reminders of the past were everywhere.

Another said,

I can picture his 'junk shop' now. Loads of old cycle parts. Black & white television amongst the junk (working). The oil stove giving off its killer fumes. The very old poster for Norwich vs. Southampton at the Nest, plus another for the Hippodrome Theatre. I asked Dodger if he ever thought of retirement, to which he answered 'Now and again...' – he was nearing 90 at the time.

I remember going in the shop to find Dodger on his knees with his tin bath half filled with water. He said 'I'll be with you in a minute' as he went all round the inner tube. And finally ... 'Bugger me, there is no puncture,' when it turned out to be just a faulty valve.

A lady called Pamela wrote in to say she recognised herself as the rider of the bedstead bike in one of the photographs from the 1950s (Figure 86) which was taken at the rugby club field off Bishop Bridge. She said she very much hoped some kind of memorial would be put up in the city to Dodger, adding, 'Characters like him must never be forgotten.'

Figure 86 'Pamela' riding the flying bedstead at Bishopbridge Road in the 1950s, with Arthur Pestell assisting

Figure 87 The Cambridge Street shop is now residential flats, but Dodger's name lives on. Compare the view in Figure 67.

Clearing out the shop

With Percy gone, the shop at 128 Cambridge Street remained closed up on Elsie's instructions, with only close family members allowed to visit. Clearing out the property was a drawn-out process. The newer stock (such as Raleigh Chopper bikes still in their packaging) could be found a home, but there were many older bikes, some of them welded together with rust. And of course a mountain of parts and accessories of various ages, plus certain wartime items you would not expect to find in a bike shop.

The shop was eventually auctioned in June 1996 (as was Percy's Adelaide Street house) and sold to a builder for conversion into flats. That it had previously been Dodger's premises was immortalised in a penny-farthing wall plate prominently displayed on the Cambridge Street frontage (Figure 87 and back cover). Little do most passers-by know that Dodger's stay at that particular location was only the last two decades of a century-long history within the neighbourhood.

Dispersal of cycle collection

In Percy's will he bequeathed his collection of 'old time cycles, motor cycles and trick cycles' to Elsie, expressing the hope that she would 'ultimately pass them on to some member of the family who will appreciate them'. Most of the machines were being kept in sheds along with motorcycles and other items at Allen's Lane.[39]

---

39 Two rusting motorcycles had previously been recovered from outbuildings at Sunnyside, Wymondham.

Those vintage bicycles that avoided being stolen during occasional break-ins were eventually transported to the first National Cycle Museum at Lincoln. This closed after two years, then the collection was stored in a hangar at RAF Scampton. It was made known at Elsie's funeral in 1999 that the bicycles had just been moved to the new location of the national cycle collection at Llandrindod Wells, Powys.

A note on the Kerrison inheritance

The deaths first of Percy in 1995, and then Elsie in 1999, marked the end of Dodger's dynasty. Certainly the cycle shop had closed for the very last time, and it was that tangible outlet which had sustained the story through the final decades.

We may ask why could not have Dodger's continued as a business, and what became of that family inheritance?

The answers are not simple. They lie within the 'frailty of human nature that never changes',[40] in the unexpectedness of circumstances, and in the prejudices and pride that inhabit all groups and families.

We have noted how while George Henry Kerrison was born into poverty, his natural drive took him out of it through sheer hard work and ability to exploit the opportunities of providing for the needs of the society around. For many years his sons Percy and Freddie continued the growth of the empire, both before and after the unfortunate death of their father. It was that event that must, if anything, have contributed to a stubborn single-mindedness that was later honed during the decade of struggle against a heavy-handed city council.

As time went on, the cycle business increasingly centred around Percy, helped by his sister Elsie, these being the only two siblings who had not married. There were no direct descendants to take over the firm. Freddie's death at a relatively early age only consolidated the power into the hands of those two. Differences of personality and outlook that are common within any family perhaps became more entrenched within the wider Dodger dynasty, in particular leading to an alienation of Freddie's branch of the family from Percy, Elsie and May, and to a lesser extent the marginalisation of Emily's branch of the tree.

In the absence of a visible successor, and with the younger

---

40 This expression was suggested by Dawn and is attributed to Marcus Aurelius.

(i.e. third) generation not invited in but preferring to make their way elsewhere, it could be argued the family firm lost its forward drive and began to stagnate. The cycle business was barely functioning for the last 15 to 20 years of Percy's life, and certainly not generating any value for investment in the future, even if anyone of vision had been given the opportunity to turn things around. Some late-stage approaches by outsiders for the business and goodwill were rebuffed by Percy and Elsie.

Much of the real estate acquired before and immediately after the Second World War had been lost (compulsorily sold at rock-bottom prices) during the moves of the 1950s and 1960s, and what was left in the portfolio was not managed in the most effective or timely way. Valuable bicycles and numerous other items that had been stored deteriorated over time, and some were stolen. Percy and Elsie's final years in residential care further depleted the financial residue. Although various family members received a share of Elsie's residual estate, she had rewritten her will before she died and made a series of generous bequests to outside organisations.

And the Chapel Street site today? That place of such busy activity over many decades is now covered in part by a car parking space adjacent to the 1960s Bishop Herbert House, by other buildings and by the concrete slabs of a pedestrian area (Figure 88). The street is remembered only in the name of Chapel Walk

Figure 88 Elevated eastern view today directly along the line of former Chapel Street towards Union Street (as marked on Figure 3)

Figure 89 The name of the walkway recalls
Chapel Street which ran nearby

(Figure 89), a thoroughfare which runs some 10 metres north of (but parallel to) the original street line (i.e. through the rear yards of nos. 16–30, the previous buildings shown on Figure 31).

These days, few of the residents of the area will have heard of Dodger's or of the Kerrisons. Yet this was indisputably a powerful and popular local family in its time. This book is an attempt to assimilate and condense a large archive of papers, images and memories, and it is hoped the setting down of this account will allow the legend of the dynasty to live on.

9

In the context of other
Norwich cycle businesses

The story of Dodger's is remarkable and interesting in itself, but there are parallel stories that could be told of other long-standing family businesses involved in providing for the many cyclists of Norwich.

One way of tracing the development of the local cycling economy across the city is to look through trade directories such as *Kelly's* and earlier listings. These enable us to get a feel for the number and geographical spread of cycle shops and related businesses, and how this changed over time.

It should however be borne in mind that simple listings provide little information on the size or importance of the particular concern, and it is also likely that some dealers were not interested in being listed, perhaps because of registration or subscription issues. This became apparent when researching the entry for Dodger's, which was recorded as 'Kerrison G H & P' until about 1950, then 'Dodger's' until the early 1960s, but subsequently disappeared from the list even though we know Percy was still very much trading.[41]

---

41 He appears again in the Thomson Directories of the 1980s.

Figure 90 Delivery of bikes from railway station to Willmott's Cycle store, Prince of Wales Road, early 1930s

The 1911 *Jarrold's Directory* listed five 'cycle manufacturers', being Kirby (St Benedict's), Walter Morris (Prince of Wales Road), Roworth Bros. (Back of the Inns), Whitfield (Bethel Street) and Willmott Bros. (Prince of Wales Road, see Figure 90).

Compare that with the 1924 *Kelly's Directory* which lists a total of 29 'cycle agents & dealers' which includes some notable Norwich names such as Fielding's (three addresses), Halford (Magdalen Street) and Pratt's (St Giles). Separately listed in that year are nine further firms under 'cycle accessories', 'cycle engineers', 'cycle factors' and 'cycle repairers'. Interestingly, the listing includes no mention of Lusher's of King Street, with whom George Kerrison had made contact in 1921.

Moving forward to 1934 we find 46 'cycle agents & dealers'

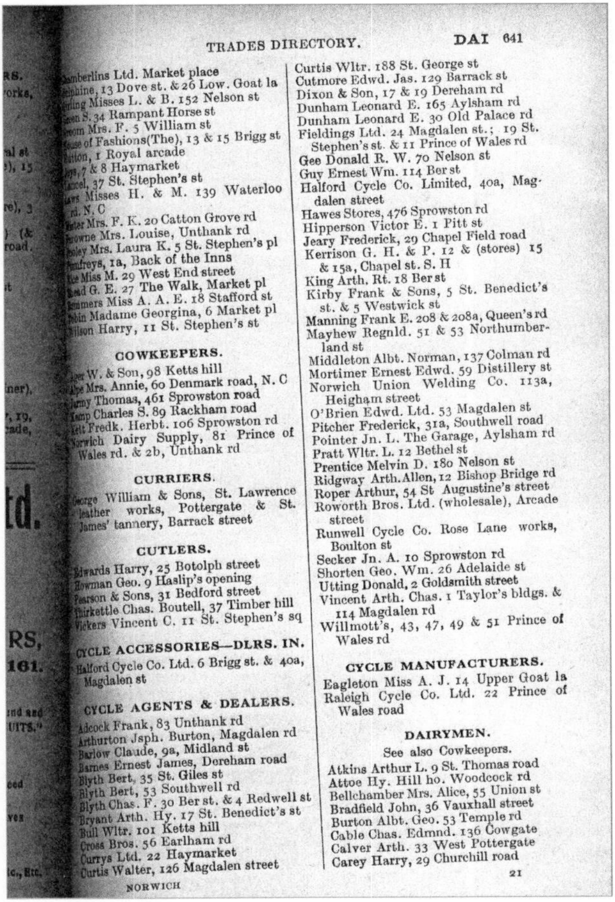

Figure 91
Kelly's Directory
listing of cycle
agents and
dealers in
Norwich, 1934

TRADES DIRECTORY.   DAI 641

...berlins Ltd. Market place
...haine, 13 Dove st. & 26 Low. Goat la
...ling Misses L. & B. 152 Nelson st
...n S. 34 Rampant Horse st
...om Mrs. F. 5 William st
...use of Fashions(The), 13 & 15 Brigg st
...ton, 1 Royal arcade
..., ? & 8 Haymarket
..., 37 St. Stephen's st
...are Misses H. & M. 139 Waterloo
...ri, N.C
...der Mrs. F. K. 20 Catton Grove rd
...owne Mrs. Louise, Unthank rd
...aley Mrs. Laura K. 5 St. Stephen's pl
...mfreys, 1a, Back of the Inns
...ree Miss M. 29 West End street
...and G. E. 27 The Walk, Market pl
...semers Miss A. A. E. 18 Stafford st
...bin Madame Georgina, 6 Market pl
...lson Harry, 11 St. Stephen's st

COWKEEPERS.
...ee W. & Son, 98 Ketts hill
...lye Mrs. Annie, 60 Denmark road, N. C
...rmy Thomas, 461 Sprowston road
...amp Charles S. 89 Rackham road
...ett Fredk. Herbt. 106 Sprowston rd
...rwich Dairy Supply, 81 Prince of Wales rd & 2b, Unthank rd

CURRIERS.
...eorge William & Sons, St. Lawrence leather works, Pottergate & St. James' tannery, Barrack street

CUTLERS.
...wards Harry, 25 Botolph street
...owman Geo. 9 Haslip's opening
...earson & Sons, 31 Bedford street
...hirkettle Chas. Boutell, 37 Timber hill
...ickers Vincent C. 11 St. Stephen's sq

CYCLE ACCESSORIES—DLRS. IN.
...alford Cycle Co. Ltd. 6 Brigg st. & 40a, Magdalen st

CYCLE AGENTS & DEALERS.
...dcock Frank, 83 Unthank rd
...rthurton Jsph. Burton, Magdalen rd
...arlow Claude, 9a, Midland st
...James Ernest James, Dereham road
...lyth Bert, 35 St. Giles st
...lyth Bert, 53 Southwell rd
...lyth Chas. F. 30 Ber st. & 4 Redwell st
...ryant Arth. Hy. 17 St. Benedict's st
...ull Wltr. 101 Ketts hill
...ross Bros. 56 Earlham rd
...urrys Ltd. 22 Magdalen street
...urtis Walter, 126 Magdalen street

NORWICH

Curtis Wltr. 188 St. George st
Cutmore Edwd. Jas. 129 Barrack st
Dixon & Son, 17 & 19 Dereham rd
Dunham Leonard E. 165 Aylsham rd
Dunham Leonard E. 30 Old Palace rd
Fieldings Ltd. 24 Magdalen st.; 19 St. Stephen's st. & 11 Prince of Wales rd
Gee Donald R. W. 70 Nelson st
Guy Ernest Wm. 114 Ber st
Halford Cycle Co. Limited, 40a, Magdalen street
Hawes Stores, 476 Sprowston rd
Hipperson Victor E. 1 Pitt st
Jeary Frederick, 29 Chapel Field road
Kerrison G. H. & P. 12 & (stores) 15 & 15a, Chapel st. S. H
King Arth. Rt. 18 Ber st
Kirby Frank & Sons, 5 St. Benedict's st. & 5 Westwick st
Manning Frank E. 208 & 208a, Queen's rd
Mayhew Regnld. 51 & 53 Northumberland st
Middleton Albt. Norman, 137 Colman rd
Mortimer Ernest Edwd. 59 Distillery st
Norwich Union Welding Co. 113a, Heigham street
O'Brien Edwd. Ltd. 53 Magdalen st
Pitcher Frederick, 31a, Southwell road
Pointer Jn. L. The Garage, Aylsham rd
Pratt Wltr. L. 12 Bethel st
Prentice Melvin D. 180 Nelson st
Ridgway Arth.Allen,12 Bishop Bridge rd
Roper Arthur, 54 St Augustine's street
Roworth Bros. Ltd. (wholesale), Arcade street
Runwell Cycle Co. Rose Lane works, Boulton st
Secker Jn. A. 10 Sprowston rd
Shorten Geo. Wm. 26 Adelaide st
Utting Donald, 2 Goldsmith street
Vincent Arth. Chas. 1 Taylor's bldgs. & 114 Magdalen rd
Willmott's, 43, 47, 49 & 51 Prince of Wales rd

CYCLE MANUFACTURERS.
Eagleton Miss A. J. 14 Upper Goat la
Raleigh Cycle Co. Ltd. 22 Prince of Wales road

DAIRYMEN.
See also Cowkeepers.
Atkins Arthur L. 9 St. Thomas road
Attoe Hy. Hill ho. Woodcock rd
Bellchamber Mrs. Alice, 55 Union st
Bradfield John, 36 Vauxhall street
Burton Albt. Geo. 53 Temple rd
Cable Chas. Edmnd. 136 Cowgate
Calver Arth. 33 West Pottergate
Carey Harry, 29 Churchill road

21

(Figure 91) which now includes Bryant's (St Benedict's) and Mayhew's (Northumberland Street), plus two 'cycle manufacturers', being Raleigh (Prince of Wales Road) and Miss A J Eagleton (Upper Goat Lane). There is no mention here of motor cycle firm Johnson, Burton & Theobold Ltd who produced the Norwich Rival bicycle in the late 1930s. By the time of the 1954 directory, the number on the list had reduced slightly to 40.

By contrast, the 1975 edition of *Kelly's Directory* has only 13 'cycle agents & dealers' which now includes the familiar names Freeman's (Heigham Street), Curry's (St Stephen's Street) and Dixon's (Waterloo Road). In later years the list included some notable independent local dealers including John Borwell Cycles of Knowsley Road, and Specialised Cycles of Connaught Road which was previously located at Cambridge Street very close to Dodger's.

Today we would count four or five large bike retailers located in the city centre (most of them branches of national or regional chains) plus about eight to ten smaller bike shops farther out of the city, which still include a handful of traditional family-owned businesses.

One of these is Freeman's, who proudly display the words 'established family business since 1896' above their shop-front

Figure 92
Frank Kirby
Senior outside
his shop in
St Benedict's
Street, early
years of
twentieth
century

Figure 93
The late Ray
Freeman
and Richard
Freeman
behind the
counter, around
2010

in Heigham Street. This actually refers to the firm founded by
Frank Kirby Senior in St Benedict's (Figure 92), in premises
which included a forge in the basement. It was later taken over
by his son Frank Kirby Junior, who lived with his family above
the shop and developed it into one of the top bike shops in the
city by the middle of the century. Frank's son David was a car-
penter, but eventually took over the running of the business in
1955 as the third generation, while his daughter Mary went to
work for the Raleigh Cycle Company in Norwich.

It was Mary who met and married Ray Freeman. He joined
Kirby's and opened their second shop in Heigham Street, which
fairly soon afterwards became independent from Kirby in 1962,
trading as Ray Freeman Cycles. Although the premises were
quite small, he developed his business into a force to be reck-
oned with in the 1960s and 1970s, selling large numbers of
imported Puch and Emmelle cycles.

Ray's son Richard joined the family business in 1977 (Figure
93), and he and wife Joy took over completely in 1991, continuing to make their way by selling new ranges of utility and
sports cycles but also capitalising on the firm's traditional
strengths in service and repairs. By 2006, their son Matt had
helped launch a website and hence develop a strong online presence ahead of other retailers, and soon after, daughter Laura
joined the firm as the next generation, still in the original shop.

Bryant's cycle shop was a few doors further along St
Benedict's Street from Kirby's, now remembered only as the
name of the café bar The Bicycle Shop. This was another family
business spanning three generations. It was established in 1918

by Arthur Bryant, and continued by his son Les, specialising in more sporty bicycles than the shop along the road, even further from the sector of the market served by Dodger's. The firm was wound up by his son Chris Bryant in 2000, and much of the shop's historic memorabilia that was in store were sadly lost in a fire in 2007.

Other similar stories of local family cycle businesses could be told, reflecting the intensity of activity during the heyday of Norwich's cycling economy.

10

Always a cycling city

Why Norwich?

Norwich is an ancient city with a long history stretching back many centuries before the invention of the bicycle. But it would be true to say that the city did embrace the bike at an early stage in the machine's existence, and cycling has remained important here – more than in most other cities on this side of the North Sea. We can identify a number of possible reasons why Norwich has always been a cycling city.

One reason could be the relative mildness of the topography, in that the city and surroundings are hardly mountainous terrain. Having said that, Norwich is one of the hillier cities in southern England, so there must be more to it than that.[42]

Many places in the UK took to the bicycle when it first appeared, but in most cities the habitual use of bikes for utility purposes died away after half a century in parallel with the growth of motor traffic. However, it seems that cycling fared less badly in Norwich than elsewhere. This was perhaps because of the social make-up of the city, including relatively large numbers of poorer residents following decades of inward migration from rural areas. Another possible reason we can identify is the city's strong historic and cultural connection with the more austere outlook common in the Low Countries, where cycling also remained persistently important at a time when it was on the wane elsewhere.

A further factor to bear in mind is that the appearance of the bicycle by chance coincided with a time when Norwich was undergoing a very rapid geographical expansion. The city didn't start extending beyond the medieval walled city until the early part of the nineteenth century. As this process accelerated towards the end of the century the bicycle must have quickly become an attractive option for getting around the growing city, when it was no longer necessarily the case that everything remained within a comfortable walking distance.[43]

---

42 There is an annual organised race up Gas Hill, a challenging 30-metre climb from Riverside to the high ground of Thorpe Hamlet, at a gradient varying between 1 in 8 and 1 in 5½.

43 Dodger's was by coincidence based in one of those areas where the earliest sub-

Figure 94 Percy Kerrison and one of his boneshakers (the pedals have been removed) dating from the 1860s

Figure 95 Ticket for one of the early annual dinners of Norwich Amateur Bicycle Club, founded in 1879

A *relatively recent invention*

It is easy to overlook how historically recent was the invention and development of the bicycle. It wasn't until 1817 that the first steerable version of a dandy-horse appeared, which worked a bit like a modern child's balance bike. Then in 1839 a Scottish blacksmith added treadles so you could keep your feet off the ground. In 1861 the first pedals were invented, attached to the front wheel, to create the original velocipede or 'boneshaker', which shortly afterwards was put into mass production (Figure 94).

The first 'penny farthings' (high-wheelers) came along in 1870, followed by increasingly rapid technical innovation, driven by a sudden but relatively short-lived bicycling craze amongst their upper-class owners. Once the newly invented chain became used around 1879 allowing gearing, smaller-diameter wheels could be used and so we soon arrived at the form of 'safety bicycle' we know today, epitomised by the Rover Safety built by John Starley in 1885.

The key technological components of spoked wheels, ball

urban development had occurred, the age of which was one reason for the relatively poor condition of the housing in the Chapel Street area compared with other suburban areas.

bearing races, pneumatic tyres and derailleur gears all appeared in that 1870–90s period, culminating in a mass-produced machine that offered unprecedented personal mobility at modest cost. That suited the lower-middle classes for day-to-day journeying, as well as playing its part in the emancipation of women in the period before the First World War.

Across the UK there followed what could be termed a half-century long period of 'cycling normality', where the bicycle took on an unremarkable (but essential) role as a means of normal transport. That continued right up to 1950, after the Second World War, when the end of fuel rationing triggered the mass motoring craze.

Cycling in Norwich

The city was at the forefront of the nation's enthusiasm for bicycles in those early days. It was a Mr Thorn of St Giles Gate, Norwich who first introduced the 'Paris Velocipede' to the eastern counties in 1869, and that year the Norwich Velocipede Club was formed, with demonstrations in the Corn Hall and Chapelfield. Following the arrival of high-wheelers, the Norwich Amateur Bicycle Club was formed as early as 1879 (Figure 95). The East Anglian Cycle Club appeared rather later, in 1921, founded primarily for rides, tours and racing (usually on bikes with dropped handlebars), and was one of the largest such clubs in the country (Figure 96).

The national body Cyclists' Touring Club had been formed in 1878 as the Bicycle Touring Club, and the name-change occurred in 1882 following the suggestion of a 'Mr L. Samuel of Norwich', as recorded in the CTC minutes.[44]

The craze of cycle racing in the 1880s and 1890s had led to the development of many arenas and velodromes in Britain, many of which later became football grounds. In Norwich we had a quarter-mile track at the Recreation Ground off Earlham Road. This was constructed with properly banked corners, the undulating remnants of which are still visible to the rear of school buildings today, and there was also a large timber stand for spectators backing onto the rear boundary of Earlham House.

This track was the scene of fierce two-wheeled competition in tightly organised events from around 1880 through to the

---

44 We don't know much more about Mr Samuel. The CTC only changed its name again in 2016, to Cycling UK.

Figure 96 An East Anglian Cycle Club ride passes along Upper King Street in the 1920s

1930s, on racing bicycles and occasionally tandems (Figure 97). One of the later champion competitors of the 1930s was Len Woods, a national time trial record holder, who went on to be a well-known Norfolk policeman.

Aside from the sporting cycle activities, there is much evidence pointing to the importance of cycling to Norwich for normal transport purposes right up to and after the Second World War. There is an arresting nineteenth-century photograph (see Figure 98) of a group of ten or so people and eight bikes (including a ladies three-wheeler sociable) all crammed in the front garden of an end terrace house in Alexandra Road, which at the time was Ducker's Dairy.

Many workers used bikes as part of their job, often adapted to carry cargo. Public-sector workers such as postmen and policemen used bikes as a matter of course. Most photographs showing street scenes include numerous people riding bikes amongst the horse-drawn and later motor vehicles, and of

Figure 97 Race start at the Recreation Road Ground, 1930s. Earlham House lies behind the pavilion, and some of the track banking survives today. On the right is champion rider Len Woods.

Figure 98 Assembled cyclists ouside Ducker's Dairy, 130 Alexandra Road, probably 1890s

course negotiating hazardous tram lines in the city centre during the period 1899–1935 (Figure 99). It is not surprising that such a key component of the economy provided local business for Dodger's and so many other cycle dealers.

Bicycles particularly came into their own during and immediately after the Second World War because of the shortage of fuel, their suitability for negotiating bomb-damaged streets and the general state of austerity.

It is the photographs of the late 1940s and early 1950s that seem to show the greatest density of bicycle users. Soon after that the streets became increasingly dominated by motor vehicles (Figure 100) which quickly filled up the road-space that had been created by widening for trams or following

Figure 99 Avoiding trams and tram lines in Orford Place, around 1930

Figure 100 Cyclists still formed a significant part of the traffic flow in 1957, pictured at the top of Prince of Wales Road

clearance of old or damaged buildings. The next three decades were dominated by transport planning based on the vision of a 'motor city' that seemed to offer a brave new world of personal car travel, and this led to further serious damage to the city's heritage through road widening and construction of incomplete sections of inner ring road.

Any account of Norwich as a cycling city must include mention of Norwich Cycling Campaign, which was formed in 1990 through the coming together of bike users and environmentalists wanting to promote the notion that cycling was part of the answer to the city's present and future transport challenges, rather than a throwback to the past. The early days of this group was built

Figure 101 Norwich Cycling Campaign stunt to highlight the folly of trying to route Norwich's cycle network up Gas Hill, 1990

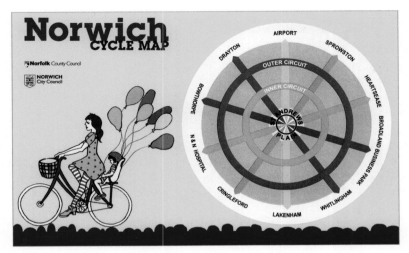

Figure 102 Graphics used on the Norwich Cycle Map of 2016, based on the colour-coded Pedalways

around various stunts and demonstrations designed to make their point (Figure 101).

Over the following quarter-century this voluntary group witnessed a gradual winning of the argument. The attitudes of local decision-makers slowly changed from wanting to deter or just tolerate cycling (during the 1970s and 1980s), through indifference or even pity towards cyclists (in the 1990s and 2000s) right through to encouragement and hopefully acceptance today – recognition that cycling is just a normal activity for a modern European city.

In 2013 Norwich was successful in bidding to central government for a Cycle City Ambition Grant of several million pounds which was followed by a second round of significant funding a few years later. This has been used to develop the 'Pedalways' cycle network featuring a range of expensive cycle infrastructure and other measures (Figure 102), working with wider measures including serious traffic reduction in the city centre.

The Pedalways project has been associated with controversy locally, not least because of an awkward and unresolved question as to whether bicycles should comfortably be part of the traffic on the highway, or should be segregated from it. It is interesting to note that this was essentially the same discussion being had during the cycling craze of over a century ago.

A recent development is the arrival on Norwich streets of

several hundred bright yellow bicycles forming a fleet for hire using a smartphone-based app. Unlike previous hire schemes, the bikes are station-free and can conveniently be used (at a cost) from any origin to any destination within a defined area. The Beijing-based company behind the hire bikes clearly perceived the city as one of the earlier UK candidates for launching the platform.

Those who believe in promoting cycling point out that having more people habitually making their local journeys by bicycle is good for the whole community – including those not on bikes – and supports a sense of a civilised place. In British terms Norwich has always been, and always will be, a cycling city. The Dodgers' story is but a part of that transportation inheritance.

References

Most of the material in this book was obtained from the private archive of papers and photographs held by family members, but reference was also made to the following sources:

- British Pathé film: *The Norwich Dodgers Penny Farthing Club* www.britishpathe.com/video/cycles
- *Norfolk at the Pictures* – Cinemaplus/Archant publication pp.16–19
- *Norwich Cycling Campaign archive 1990–2015* www.norwichcyclingcampaign.org/newsletters/
- *Analysis of Norwich municipal architecture in the 1960s: Norwich Council Housing, 1955–74: David Percival and 'Regional Architectural Tradition,* https://municipaldreams. wordpress.com/2015/09/29/norwich_architectural_tradition
- *Norwich in the Nineteenth Century,* edited by Christopher Barringer, Gliddon Books, 1984
- *The Penguin Book of the Bicycle,* Roderick Watson and Martin Gray, 1978

Picture sources and credits

All pictures have been sourced from the Kerrison family's collection except for the following:

Front and rear covers main pictures: courtesy of British Pathé.
Figures 2 and 3: drawn by Matthew Williams.
Figures 5, 21, 36, 60, 74, 80, 87, 88 and 89: photographs by Matthew Williams.
Figures 4, 43, 63, 78 and 101: courtesy Archant – *Eastern Evening News*.
Figures 8, 35 and 37: photographs by George Plunkett, courtesy of Jonathan Plunkett.
Figures 13, 79, 85, 90, 99 and 100: courtesy of Archant/EDP library.
Figures 32, 95, 96, 97 and 98: courtesy of Norfolk County Council Library and Information Service. Enjoy thousands of images of Norfolk's unique history at www.picture.norfolk. gov.uk
Figures 92 and 93: courtesy of Freeman Cycles.
Figure 102: courtesy of Norwich City Council.

The authors, editor and publisher have made every effort to ensure that all necessary permissions have been obtained for the material reproduced in this book. Grateful thanks are due to organisations and individuals who have given these permissions. If any omissions are brought to our attention, we will be happy to rectify them in any future edition.

Appendix I

Advertising rhymes

What follows is a selection of fifteen rhymes that appeared on Dodger signboards and/or handbills. They are arranged in roughly chronological order.

There is uncertainty as to exactly who wrote these, and evidence that some were amended from the earlier versions (e.g. compare the two versions of 'The greatest treasure').

The earliest handwritten verses were penned by a character named William Earl, who styled himself Norfolk Bill. Old Dodger probably wrote some of the earlier slogans, Percy attempted at least one rhyme ('At Dodger's shop'), Elsie wrote a later one ("'Tis true it was the Council'), and June produced some of the later poems.

As a busy shopping centre, 'tis not
like "Market Place".
What Chaple Street can boast of:—
your wants it can replace.
We've Oil, Firewood, -and coal,
Props— Pea-sticks to dis-gorge—
So hurry up! and clear me out—
Says, Poor Old George!

I'm Coming! Trade's Humming!
My sheds I must dis-gorge,
Or I'll have "The Watch-dogs" biting
Me— I'm Poor Old George!

"This World is but a City, with many a
crooked Street—
And we who live in Crook's Place— The
down-and-outs we meet.
From early morn till late at night,
we're working -at our forge.
Those in need oft' call upon us—
Poor Old George!

I'm Coming! Trade's Humming!
My Place I must dis-gorge—
I can hear the Guardians sympathising
Poor Old George!

Once this was a thriving FIRM.
I could, sit down at my ease.
And chop my sticks, from dawn to
dusk—
And earn my bread -and cheese,
But, now to give two foot more
air
My store I must dis-gorge
Well Where will you look for
Antiques now, says
Poor old George!

I'm Coming! Trade's booming! I have
no flameless forge,
I'm ever out to serve you well, says
Poor old George!

So, now, kind friends, please rally
round me in my hour of need—
And visitors to Norwich can
satisfy their greed,
For Curios you need not seek, all
please I'll afford—
And everything a motorist need—
I keep it— Poor Old George.

I'm Coming! Trade's Humming!
But my cellers I'd dis-gorge!
Or the Beagles will be wolfing of
me— Poor Old George!

W. Earl.

The Royal Standard Cycle Stores.

The greatest treasure the World can hold
Search - as you will - End to end
It is not power, fame, gems or gold,
But just the use of a friend.

And if you'd travel in comfortable ease
By highway, byeway or dithe;
There's nought to compare in this hemisphere
With - a reliable BIKE.

Hercules

A Hercules BIKE is a worker's true friend -
None can excel it for All-weather wear -
Buy one - And ride one - We recommend -
Then ride in safety for many a year.

You need not: "CASH DOWN" - "PAY AS YOU RIDE!"
"THREE PENCE PER DAY" - You'll never miss -
"SAFE AS THE BANK" - Or aught else beside -
No worry pending - "Isn't this bliss?"

Britain's Best Bicycle! - Suitably named
Strong as Hercules! - Samson out-vied.
Made in Birmingham, yet its World-famed.
Good for - a life-time, none have denied.

A "Mass lines production" - That's why its cheap!
Speeds up employment - Expanding each year.
If seeking enjoyment: - "Sow, and you'll reap."
Life long satisfaction by purchasing here.

DODGERS

Established over 60 years

TELEPHONE 22499

Where your Grandfather learnt to ride a cycle

THE ONLY CYCLE FIRM IN NORWICH WITH

DAY AND NIGHT SERVICE

●

The greatest treasure the world can hold
Search as you will from end to end
It is not power, fame, gem or gold,
But just the use of a friend.

And if you'd ride in comfortable ease
By highway, by-way or dyke,
There's nought to compare in this hemisphere,
With a reliable lady's or gent's bike.

A trustworthy bike is a worker's true friend,
None can excel it for all weather wear.
Buy one and ride one, we recommend
You'll ride in safety for many a year.

Safe as the bank or aught else beside,
No worry pending isn't this bliss.
So if seeking enjoyment, sow and you'll reap
Life long satisfaction by purchasing here.

100 YEARS OF CYCLING—1851 MODELS TO 1951 MODELS
SEE THEM AT DODGERS

Repairs to any make of Cycle
Any make of New Cycle supplied— CASH, CREDIT OR ON HIRE

15 CHAPEL STREET - NORWICH

THE ROYAL STANDARD CYCLE DEPOT.

GIVE TOFFS THIER WINE & TOPERS BEER
HEALTH, WEALTH & ALL SOON DISAPPEAR.

AND IF YOU'R SEEKING HEALTH TODAY
NEED YOU GO FURTHER ON YOUR WAY?
DELIGHTFUL RIDES IN COUNTRY AIR

PROVIDES THAT WEALTH OF HEALTH SO DEAR

KIND FRIENDS YOU'ALL FIND WITHIN OUR STORE
EVERYTHING YOU'LL NEED
REMOUNTS, NEW MOUNTS PETROL, PARTS
REQUIRED FOR GRACE OR SPEED
INCOME NEED NOT WORRY YOU
SINCE WE GIVE CREDIT GALORE
OR IF YOU LIKE WE TAKE CASH DOWN
NOW COULD YOU WISH FOR MORE?

COVENTRY, EAGLES & HERCULES
YOU'LL FIND FOR CASH OR CREDIT
CYCLES FLEET SO TRIM & NEAT
LENT OUT, SENT OUT EACH MINUTE
EVERY ACCESSORY YOU MAY NEED

AWAIT YOU AT OUR XXXXX GARAGE
GENTS, LADIES & ALL CHILDRENS BIKES
EVEN TO A BABY CARRIAGE
NO TRANSPORT OFFICER TO FUME OR SHOUT
TO YOU LIKE OLD SIR RODGER
SATISFACTION IN EVERY TRANSACTION.

IS THE MOTTO OF OLD DODGER.

A NEW YEAR'S APPRECIATION OF MR. PERCY HARRISON, CYCLE SALESMAN AND REPAIRER.

By a Well-Satisfied Customer.

"Our PERCY" is a fellow with a smile upon his face,
And a word of cheery greeting as he goes about "Crook's Place,"
He devotes his time and effort from an early morning start,
To serve the folk and talking what is nearest to his heart.
He lives a life of service and he gains a host of friends,
For he's never actuated by base and selfish ends.

Each day he waits on people with the only thought in mind,
Of the good that he is doing, of the prospects he can find.
He raises living standards with the things he has to sell,
As he calls all folk's attention to his goods without a bell.
He never stoops to offer any piece of merchandise
That will not perform a service consistent with its price.

He meets all competition with a friendly, kindly word,
And he never speaks with malice of the things that he has heard.
He is sure the thing he's selling brings a lasting benefit,
Far greater than the profit he makes in selling it.
He's secure in his conviction that his effort is worth while
So he buckles in each morning with an everlasting smile,
Bringing work to cycle factories whose families depend
On the daily sales production of their genial, happy friend.

W. Earl.

DODGERS,

15, Chapel Street, Norwich.

Established over 60 years.

Where your Grandfather learnt to ride a cycle.

The only Cycle firm in Norwich with DAY AND NIGHT SERVICE

Come all ye lads and lassies if you've a mind for fun,
At your village feasts or galas we can show you how 'tis done.
We've the Old-time Penny-farthing Bikes, we've also Bantams, too,
And that nobby little bike that's called the Kangaroo.

We've the first Model Safety which Dad rode in days of yore.
A Dandy-cart or Hobby-horse, we've also many more.
We lend these crocks on hire for your galas or procession,
Which will demonstrate to young and old the rate of world's progression.

So when your Club Feast comes along just visit Dodgers Store,
We've Bikes of all descriptions to suit both rich and poor.
We've Gramophones and Records for the dance upon the green,
Or Portables in Radio to charm the Village Queen.

We've Flash-lamps and Batteries to guide you on your way
When you are trundling homeward after a perfect day.
We'll mend at any time your car, your bike or pram—of work we never tire.
Pay as you ride—our terms are these: cash, credit or on hire.

When your coalman cannot supply you, Dodgers will oblige you
With stones of coal and logs of wood for your fire.

Linen Props, Posts, and Rustic Wood.

Bundles of Firewood, two for One Penny.

Paraffin Oil, Electric House Lamps, and Gas Mantles always stocked.

G. H. & P. KERRISON

Cycle and Motor Cycle Agents and Repairers

12, 15 & 15a, CHAPEL STREET
Rupert Street, Norwich

The New "Chapel Street Cycle Emporium."

Have you seen the new extension to " CHAPEL ST. EMPORIUM"?
Where buyers, ah! and sellers too, get justice AD VELOREM?
" Small profits and quick returns," has been " Old Dodger's" aim
These many years he's been in trade, he's always " Played the Game."

Tho' some there are who'd "Queer his pitch," at times they find it true
When " Punctured" by adversity he'll always see you through,
From early morn till late at night, folks rally round his store,
In cars, on bikes, with prams or pails, he serves both rich and poor.

Here's "Tar" and " Creosote" held in stock, resisting storms or showers
And " Rustic-wood" of quaint design for garden seats or bowers.
For Ma, there's Linen-posts or Props, Pram-wheels or Parts and Tyres
With coal and coke, wood split or logs to replenish kitchen fires.

Accumulators he'll re-charge for you upon the spot,
Or should you need accessories in stock, he holds the lot.
In Gramophones, and Records too, you'll find it's hard to beat
The many examples he can show at his store in Chapel Street.

There's batteries for your flash-lamps to guide you on your way.
Whilst Free Concerts on the Radio are rendered while you stay.
We'll mend your bike at any time, for of work we never tire.
" Pay as you ride" Our terms are these :—Cash, Credit, or On Hire!

If you care to call and see his stock I know you will agree,
" Old Dodger's" out to bring about the best for you or me.
So, if there's blame for playing the game, who fits the cap may wear it.
But if there's any credit, just come along and share it.

ALWAYS OPEN   SERVICE THAT SATISFIES

The Betta-way Service Press, Order Office—7 Rupert St. Norwich.

AT DODGERS SHOP ON ANY
DAY

Here's Phillips Raleigh AND
B.S.A

All set out for you to
see

And buy for cash or on
H.P

Hercules cycles just
the thing

For you to buy in time
for spring

Upright cycles for the
copper

And for mum the
model shopper

Go to Dodgers straight
away

Buy your bike without
delay

After that we'd like to
bet

You will not have
one regret

Of this our ancient city
You have not seen the best
Until you've found the cycle shop
That really stands the test
A cycle old — a cycle new
or is it a repair
Just take a trip to Dodgers shop
You'll find the answer there.

Compulsory Purchase of
'DODGERS'

OR

LAND GRABBING BY THE NORWICH CITY COUNCIL

IN THE YEAR 1958.

TIS TRUE IT WAS THE COUNCIL
    DODGER HAD TO FIGHT
BUT IT WAS TO ESTABLISH
    A MAN HAS HIS RIGHTS.

WHEN THE NORWICH CITY COUNCIL
    HIS LAND THEY SET OUT TO GRAB
DODGER AND THE FAMILY
    AN EXCHANGE OF LAND DID PLAN.

IT WAS A LEASEHOLD OFFER
    THE COUNCIL DID MAKE
"FREEHOLD FOR FREEHOLD"
    DODGER DID SPAKE.

"EVICT HIM" WAS THE COUNCIL'S CRY
    "HIS PLEA FOR FREEHOLD WE WILL DENY".

THERE WAS NO NEED FOR FIGHTING
    IF THE COUNCIL CHOOSE TO BE
FAIR IN THEIR DEALINGS WITH DODGER
    AS WITH OTHERS THEY HAD BEEN.

ALTHOUGH DODGER HAS HAD TO MOVE
    IN HIS BATTLES HE HAS TRIED TO PROVE
AN ENGLISHMAN'S HOME HIS CASTLE MAY NOT BE
    BUT AN ENGLISHMAN'S COUNTRY COULD
        STILL BE A DEMOCRACY.

BY HIS FIGHTS FOR RIGHT AND LIBERTY
    DODGER WILL GO DOWN IN HISTORY.

E. KERRISON.

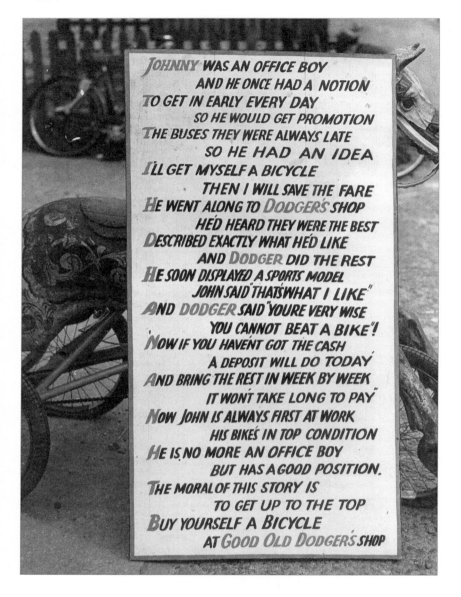

Established over 90 years   TEL: 22499

DODGER'S

Where your Grandfather learnt to ride a cycle

THE HOLIDAYS WILL SOON BE HERE
     MAKE YOURS ONE OF REAL GOOD CHEER;
COME BUY YOURSELF A NICE NEW BIKE,
     WE'VE SOMETHING YOU'RE SURE TO LIKE.

WE'VE SECONDHAND CYCLE'S TO SELL TO YOU
     WHICH BOTH PERFORM AND LOOK LIKE
                         NEW,
AT PRICES SUITABLE TO ALL,
     WHY NOT COME AND PAY A CALL?

FREE DELIVERY WE COULD ARRANGE,
     AND WILL TAKE BIKES IN PART EXCHANGE,
WITH READY CASH AND THE NEVER NEVER,
     TO MEET YOUR PURSE OUR ONE
                        ENDEAVOUR.

Raleigh   **By Hour**
Cycles   **Day**
for Hire,   **or Week**

Repairs & Accessories
Cycles & Pushchairs for Hire

DODGERS
57, SUFFOLK STREET,
NORWICH

List of old bicycles in Dodger's collection

Percy is reported to have owned up to fifty old or unusual cycles, but that does not necessarily mean they were all roadworthy at any one time. Certainly at the time of the Pathé film, there were about 25 available to participate in the cavalcade. He is seen in the film hastily preparing them to ride before they left Chapel Street.

The following is not an exclusive list but is intended to indicate the range of machines he had to choose from, together with a few brief notes on them. This has been compiled from notes kept by Percy and from numerous photographs of the bikes in action.

It is not possible to trace what happened to all of these, and it is known several of them were stolen from storage at both Cambridge Street and Allen's Lane at various stages before and after Percy's death.

Historic cycles

- Wooden tricycle or dandy-cart (probably early 1800s). Extreme left of Figure 50.
- Velocipede or boneshaker (c.1867), French made (Figure 94). At least two of these in collection.
- A selection of Ordinaries or penny farthings, sizes varying from 46 to 54 inch. Earliest is Ariel (1870), also later models by Humber (1885-7), Coventry Machinists Company and other manufacturers. Mainstay of the Penny Farthing Cycle Club (e.g. Figures 42 and 57). Included lever-driven model the Facile (Figure 61) made by Ellis & Co. in 1883.
- Rotary tricycle (approx. 1883), possibly Rudge. Asymmetric design.
- Tricycle (early 1880s) for single rider, made by Quadrant Tricycle Company.
- Kangaroo (1884) by Rudge Whitworth. Chain-driven ordinary cycle (Figure 49).
- Earliest safety bicycle – cross-framed (1886). Solid tyres.
- Approximately ten other safety bicycles (late 1800s) including

Rudge and spring-frame, mostly with solid tyres (visible on Figure 50).

- Olympia Triumph tandem tricycle (1887) by Coventry Machinists Company. Frequently ridden by Elsie and Percy in cavalcade (e.g. Figure 46).
- Bantam (1890) by Leicester Cycle Company. Geared miniature ordinary cycle (visible in Figure 46). Also a larger crypto-geared Ordinary.
- Bamboo bicycle (1896). Bamboo frame and mudguards with steel joints. Made in Holborn, and previously ridden in Norwich by Mr Shaw Tomkins. Special tyres supplied by Hurns of Norwich.
- Dursley Pederson bicycle (around 1902). English made. Cantilever 'hammock' safety cycle with original freewheel and gear.
- Other tandem tricycle – double geared, front and back (Figure 48 on right hand side).
- Sociable tricycle (side-by-side) capable of taking small third person in centre (visible in Figure 48).
- Various twentieth century roadsters of Edwardian age.
- Soldier's bicycle (WW1) with rifle mount.

Novelty cycles

- Bedstead bike ('flying bedstead'). Unique and famous, made by Percy Kerrison and James Clarke in 1951 (Figure 54). Often ridden in parades by Freddie Kerrison or Arthur Pestell.
- Fairground horse mounted on tricycle, rider in jockey outfit (visible in Figure 48).
- 'Wibbly-wobbly' bike with eccentrically-spoked wheels. Still being lent out in 1980s.
- Children's tandem tricycle (1939). Turquoise blue, unwrapped from new by Ronnie Green, frequently ridden by Pestell grandchildren (visible on elevated stand in Figure 50).

List of properties owned by Percy Kerrison covered by 1952 and 1955 Compulsory Purchase Orders[45]

Albert Terrace:	Nos 1, 2, 3, 4
Chapel Street:	Nos 7, 9, 10, 12, 11, 13, 15, 15a, 16, 20, 22, 24, 26
Coach & Horses Street:	Nos 4, 18, 20
Cross Globe Street:	Nos 11, 18, 20
Globe Street:	Nos 12, 14
Manchester Street:	Nos 6, 8, 10, 12, 14, 16, 18, 20, 22, 24, 26
Salford Street:	Nos 13, 16, 17, 18, 19, 20, 21, 22, 23, 24, 25, 27, 29, 31

The total offered purchase value for the above 50 properties was £5,095, working out at an average of £110 per property, although some of the houses were valued at the time at as little as £20.

There were some other Kerrison-owned properties in the vicinity (such as in yards off Rupert Street and at Suffolk Street), and these were covered by later compulsory purchase orders.

---

45 As listed in correspondence between Aldridge & Partners and District Valuer in 1958–60.

Appendix IV

More stories from Ronnie

Downward directions

It was on Unthank Road that I had my first accident on a bike about 1938–9. I had a Dodger's children's three-wheeler trike out on my own at the age of 4 or 5. Along Essex Street I went, past the church, and from then on downhill to Unthank Road. I must have broken speed records on a child's machine and almost broke my neck as well. I went straight over Unthank Road, hit the kerb then the flint wall opposite, yet I managed to get home.

I once could recall about fifteen mishaps on bikes. Obviously at least two had to be on (or rather off) penny far-things. The first I remember was when we were on a trip to the World's End public house at Mulbarton in 1951, starting with about half a dozen of us proudly outside the railings of the old Norfolk & Norwich Hospital having our photo taken. Then we were off along Ipswich Road, and I was behind the others.

One thing you shouldn't do on a penny farthing is take your feet off the pedals, as the whole thing is fixed wheel and you cannot get your feet back on if the pedals are flying round in a blur. Well again I say you'll never learn – and when I do, it's the hard way or too late.

In those days Tuckswood estate was only in the planners' minds, with no paths, just grass embankments. Needless to say, I managed to get past the others, doing at least 30 miles an hour down the steep hill leading to the old Harford Bridge and the River Yare, except I never got that far. The big rim of the penny farthing just shattered, with no warning at all, and yet again I finished my journey in a downwards direction.

I sat up and turned around to see the others coming towards me. They too couldn't stop but went to the side of the road where they hit the embankment, all of them over the handlebars and cat-apulted over the hedges, just the bikes left in the road – yes, the main road to Ipswich. I mention that fact because it was some 20 minutes before a car came along, it was a black Ford. The driver took me back to where we'd started, but this time the other side of the railings, inside the N&N. I was only in there for half an hour, receiving two stitches in my head. I was surely very lucky considering …

I went back to 10 Chapel Street, my granny (Dodger's) house. Not long afterwards, there was a knock at the door and in came a policeman. 'I've heard someone here had an accident on the Ipswich Road' he said, to which I replied, 'I did.' 'And what vehicle were you driving?' the policeman asked, to which I replied, 'A penny farthing bike', I said. 'Now don't you be cheeky,' said the policeman. Everybody present laughed except him.

Another of my accidents on a penny farthing bike took place on the Lord Mayor's Parade. Many old-time cycles were stored up Allen's Lane off Newmarket Road. My penny farthing was decked out with red, white and blue toilet paper woven in and out of the spokes of the large front wheel. I came out of Allen's Lane onto Newmarket Road just as a brisk westerly wind was blowing. The wheel, now being like a sail, turned sharply left but I kept on and subsequently travelled, yes, in a downward direction.

The top of Chapel Street was the 'top' in as much as the street sloped, the Rupert Street end being a bit higher than the Union Street end, where there were flats built before the war. Yet another peculiar bike accident I suffered around 1954, affecting not just myself but three grown-ups. This particular cycle had three seats in a row: the middle one was intended for a youngster. Well, we proved the machine wasn't for three grown-ups. It had a long handlebar, with four handles not six, and was a three -wheeler guided by the one front wheel. The two bigger chaps sat each end and asked me to get in the middle seat. Suddenly the front wheel lifted off the ground and went above our heads, and down Chapel Street we went gathering speed. There were no paths, we veered left a bit, all three of us yelling, then hit a row of palings – these were in Manchester Street backed by a privet hedge and can be seen in some of the photos. So we proved that middle seat was indeed for a child, as I was about 20 at the time. Arthur Pestell was one of those two blokes, I always think it was his weight that must have done it.

I remember two other hair-raising occasions while on a penny farthing. Going from St Stephen's Road to St Stephen's Street, the ground sloped away on the left side and my small back wheel left the ground. And again going into Upper King Street a sudden slope, I almost crashed through Norwich Union windows had it not been a quick dismount before the sturdy railing, which is where I finished up. Those occasions were also while taking part in the Lord Mayor's parade, and it was when we were going back afterwards we got stopped by a policeman in St Stephen's for having NO LIGHTS – though it wasn't that dark. We'd been stopped before on

Gentleman's Walk for the same reason – I have a photo of us there and it wasn't dark – only gloomy.

Carnivals

Dodger's were asked to attend many carnivals or processions and garden parties. I can remember just part of one Yarmouth Carnival, being on a penny farthing and looking for something nearby to hang on to. I found myself choosing a Lacon's float – now that's a famous Yarmouth brewery and what a float to be hanging on to, as they were handing out samples of beer in bottles in those days. I know I had a few, and that's probably why I cannot remember the rest of the day.

There was also a carnival at my second home, Wymondham, which included a fun day on King's Head Meadow. Some old-time cycles were sent down from Norwich the day before the event so the locals could decide who were brave enough or foolish enough to ride them in a race. On the day it was going to be four times around King's Head Meadow. There were all kinds of old-fashioned bikes, and one race I recall involved the bedstead. This time I was on the smallest of cycles, called the Bantam bike – it was like a very small penny farthing but with pumped-up (rather than solid) tyres, racing handlebars and with the pedals set in the front wheel.

I got off to a flying start downhill to the first left-hand bend. It seems downhills have been my downfall. As I went round the bend a pedal on the front wheel touched the ground, then I touched the ground by way of a DOWNWARD DIRECTION. I had been in front at that point, and Freddie was next on a tall penny farthing. As he passed me on the deck he said, 'Do that again – the crowd enjoyed it.'

Getting round to the start again, I found chaos – very few riders had managed to set off because the bedstead's bike had toppled at the start, bringing down most of the others. Round the third bend uphill, I'd overtaken Freddie. As I rode into the second lap laughing at the melee of entangled bikes, once more down towards the first bend, I was in front. Yet again I hit the deck in a downward direction. It's funny how people can laugh at other people's misfortune.

I cannot remember the rest of the race, probably because of what followed. The Norwich team had won, and we received a prize of Gaymer's cider from the then-famous cider factory at Attleborough. On the way back to Norwich the lorry was stopped at the Kett's Oak PH just before Hethersett to celebrate the victory. The grown-ups piled into the pub, all in a joyful manner, telling us they'd bring us out each a Vimto (a popular red drink for kids at that time) and a bag of crisps.

Imagine we five or six youngsters waiting on the back of the lorry, waiting, waiting, aged around 16 or 17 – not being so forward as teenagers are today, never having tasted any alcohol – and there unattended by any grown-ups. In the middle of the lorry stood a whole crate of Gaymer's cider. Don't drink and drive is the new adage of the day. I don't know how much the driver had, but we kids did that crate of cider proud. We were making a noise all the way to Norwich – singing a song called 'Lay that pistol down, boy', but to different words, and being a bit grown up by adding a few swear words that would be considered tame today, but worse words we none of us knew then. Some of us were poor, but we were brought up proper.

Back at Chapel Street the parents of the lads were waiting for us, and the grown-ups really got it in the neck. We were all carried off the lorry – so I was told. You will see why I can't remember most of that day.

At an earlier Wymondham Carnival circa 1947, I remember watching ATS girls pillow fights on a greasy pole above a large canvas full of water. That was most enjoyable to watch, and there I too was laughing at other people's misfortune.

I'm somewhat older now (83½ in 2017). Although 60 years ago sometimes seems like a week ago, I couldn't tell you what I had for dinner two days ago.

Ronnie Green aged about 4

Index